"*Journey Through Colossi*[a]... up. I was encouraged by ev... skillful teacher and her love for Jesus exudes throughout the entire book. You will walk away with a deeper love for Jesus and a deeper knowledge on the book of Colossians."

~**JESSICA THOMPSON,** speaker and author of *How To Help Your Anxious Teen: Discovering the Surprising Sources of Their Worries and Fears* and co-author of *Give Them Grace: Dazzling Your Kids With the Love of Jesus* and *Mom, Dad...What's Sex: Giving Your Kids a Gospel-Centered View of Sex and Our Culture*

"Clear, sound biblical truths ring throughout this book as Tara opens up the book of Colossians. She thoughtfully guides the reader to the instructions contained in this Epistle in a way where we never lose sight of Jesus, who is the point of all scripture."

~**JOEL FITZPATRICK,** Pastor, Speaker, Author of *Between us Guys: Life-Changing Conversations Between Dads and Sons* and co-author of *Mom, Dad...What's Sex: Giving Your Kids a Gospel-Centered View of Sex and Our Culture*

"*Journey through Colossians* is an outstanding resource and tool for anyone who wants to grow in their knowledge of the word of God. Tara takes the deep truths of the word of God found in Paul's letter to the Colossians and presents them in a way that is clear, accessible and edifying. Everyone from the new believer to the long-time student of the word will find something to help them nurture their love for the Lord. I highly recommend this resource for use in everything from daily devotions to group bible studies."

~**DAVID WOJNICKI,** Lead Pastor at Valley Center Community Church, Valley Center, CA

journey through...

Colossians

36-Day Verse-by-Verse Devotional

• • •

TARA BARNDT

Journey Through Colossians: 36-Day Verse-by-Verse Devotional

Copyright © 2020 by Tara Barndt

Printed in the United States of America

First Printing, 2020

Cover Design by Holly Reese

Paperback ISBN: 978-1-09832-995-2

ebook ISBN: 978-1-09832-996-9

IN MEMORY OF

George "Dad" Scipione, who faithfully lived a life
glorifying and pointing to Jesus and was my reason and mentor
in becoming a Biblical counselor,

and

Harriet Calcaterra, my dear friend, mentor and prayer partner
who shared my love for studying God's Word,
made me long for heaven and was my wonderfully biased editor
for my first two books.

ACKNOWLEDGEMENTS

To my husband, Jeremy, thank you for continuing to encourage and support me in my studies and writing. I love you always.

Thank you, Mom, for sparking a love for writing in me from the time I was four years old and writing down my dictated stories. You and Dad have always cheered me on.

Thank you, Steve Strimple, for instilling in me a love for God's Word and the example of teaching it in a way that helps others "be filled with the knowledge of His will in all spiritual wisdom and understanding."

I am grateful to Dick Kaufmann, Dennis Johnson, John Frame, Peter Jones, Mark Futato and Edmund Clowney (although no longer with us) for the wisdom you shared and the humble example you set as pastors and elders at NLPC.

Thank you, Sarah Smith, Gary Risdon, Joel Fitzpatrick and Linda Craft for your editing expertise and input. You have made me and continue to make me a better writer.

Thank you to my prayer warriors. Again and again you brought me before the throne of grace in my time of need.

Thank you to my gracious heavenly Father who called me out of the domain of darkness into the kingdom of His beloved Son, in whom I have redemption, the forgiveness of sins.

TABLE OF CONTENTS

INTRODUCTION

I attended Calvin Christian High School in Escondido. There my Bible teacher instilled a passion in me to study and understand God's Word. Until my first doctrine class, I wasn't even really aware specific doctrines existed. Those classes opened a whole new world to me.

I wish I could say I have been a faithful student of Scripture since then, but as with most of us I would imagine, my quiet times of study and prayer with God have gone up and down. In my early twenties, my college and career group went through various video studies by R.C. Sproul and again I had that hunger to learn more. Knowing the depth of wisdom in Scripture has made me dissatisfied with many of the Bible studies or devotionals that are available. This doesn't mean that those don't have value, but I wanted studies that encouraged me to dig deeper into Scripture and consider how that applied to my life.

During my teens and twenties, I was also blessed to attend a church with pastors and elders who were humble, wise, Christ-like men rich in the wisdom of God. Many were professors from Westminster Seminary in California. These men's teaching and leadership along with their wives' examples encouraged me to continue growing in spiritual wisdom and to walk in a grateful manner worthy of the calling.

All these experiences led me, as I began teaching women's Bible studies, to teach verse-by-verse through Paul's letters. Now through my husband's encouragement and God's grace at work through His Holy Spirit, those Bible studies are being turned into the *Journey Through* series of devotionals.

I get excited seeing others understand and apply Scripture. I get excited each time *I* read Scripture and new things convict or encourage or just plain jump out at me. God has lavished us with the amazing gift of His Word that reveals Himself and His will for us. As Paul prayed, I pray for you as you begin this journey through Colossians, "And so, from the day we heard, we have not ceased to pray for you, asking that you may be filled with the knowledge of His will in all spiritual wisdom and understanding, so as to walk in a manner worthy of the Lord, fully pleasing to Him, bearing fruit in every good work and increasing in the knowledge of God. May you be strengthened with all power, according to His glorious might, for all endurance and patience with joy, giving thanks to the Father, who has qualified you to share in the inheritance of the saints in light." Colossians 1:9-12

As I worked through Colossians Chapter 1, I realized how much rich and foundational doctrine there is. It is key to the rest of the book of Colossians. Take extra days if needed for absorbing the truths and keep going! As you do, you'll see how those doctrines apply to you.

There are several appendices at the end of the devotional that you can use during this study to enrich the application of Colossians: Appendix A "Bible Study Questions" for using this devotional in a group setting. Appendix B "In Him" chart is to record all the places in Colossians that this phrase is used and the corresponding blessing, Appendix C "Prayers from Colossians" is for praying Scripture for others, and Appendix D "Songs from Colossians" for those who want to be reminded via music of the truths from Colossians.

DAY 1

COLOSSIANS 1:1-2

*Paul, an apostle of Christ Jesus by the will of God,
and Timothy our brother, to the saints and faithful brothers in Christ at
Colossae: Grace to you and peace from God our Father.*

For years, I have read through Paul's letters and quickly sailed over the "grace and peace" greetings. I know what grace and peace are after all, so let's get on to the real meat. Little did I know how much I was missing in those three words.

The Greek word for grace is *charis*. Grace is God's unmerited favor granted or gifted to sinful man. In Paul's greeting is a reminder of God's free gift of salvation, an exhortation to respond in thankfulness, and a prayer asking for God's abiding favor as we face daily needs and trials. We can do nothing apart from Him. What an encouragement it must have been to the Colossians to have Paul's reminder of God's grace in their salvation and sanctification. God had them covered. May it be an encouragement to you as well.

There is another similar word used thirty-eight times in the New Testament. It is *eucharisteō*, a verb meaning "to be grateful or to give thanks." It contains the word *charis* (grace). Another word based on *charis* is *chara* meaning joy (Used five times in Colossians. The verb *rejoice*, *chairō*, a favorite of Paul's in Philippians, appears two times.). Together, these three words give me a picture of a beautiful swirl of thankfulness and joy in light of God's gifts of grace, making this grace-greeting even richer.

The Greek word for *peace* is *eirene*. It is the peace or rest we have in the assurance of our salvation through Christ's atoning work alone. The Hebrew word *shalom* may be more familiar. As the Jewish people may have been in the habit of saying shalom like our hello, we can gloss over Paul's greeting without a second thought, but his words are chock-full of meaning. To say peace to someone was to wish for them a foretaste of the Messianic age to come: to be complete and whole, to be healthy, to be safe, to be prosperous, to be tranquil, to be rested, to be happy, to be free from discord or agitation. When was the last time you prayed for a brother or sister in Christ to have a foretaste of heaven?

I know—that is an abundance of Greek and definitions that may still seem like they belong in a seminary and not in your everyday life. However, those words have begun to change the way I approach my day and how I pray for others. I am learning to meditate daily on just how amazing God's grace is. Sometimes I am vividly aware of my sinfulness. On those days I sink into God's grace. I am thankful for the blessing of His undeserved grace and mercy; that He is seeing me through Jesus' righteousness not covered in my own sin. Other days I miss that log in my own eye, and I forget to show any acknowledgment or gratitude. Some days are even great. My sin seems limited to a stray thought. I've nailed righteous for a little while (probably missing a log again). But every day, good or bad, every hour, every minute, I need God's grace. All my righteousness is as filthy rags, and I am just as desperate for God and His grace in my good moments and as in my bad.

Jerry Bridges says, "The sinner does not need more grace than the saint, nor does the immature and undisciplined believer need more than the godly, zealous missionary. We all need the same amount of grace because the "currency" of our good works is debased and worthless before God."[1]

For over ten years, I have experienced chronic pain and nerve sensitivity issues; none of which doctors have figured out. I've had melanoma cancer three times (thankfully caught early). It is only by God's grace that I have experienced complete peace through these things. I can't explain it apart from God. I think of the peace I experience now through physical trials, and marvel that this is a mere drop compared to the peace we will experience in heaven in our Father's presence, free from the effects of sin in this world.

It would be easy to solely focus on the grace and peace in these verses especially as we have just seen how incredibly rich in meaning they are, but we don't want to gloss over the people even though they might be familiar. Paul is listed first as was customary for the author. Paul refers to being an apostle of Christ perhaps because he did not establish and likely never visited the church in Colossae (vs 2:1). Including this credential also established his authority was "by the will of God". Paul wrote this letter from prison about the same time as the letter to the Ephesian church, around A.D. 60.

Timothy was Paul's spiritual son and a trusted friend. He joined Paul during Paul's second missionary journey, stayed by his side during imprisonment and helped establish the churches in Philippi, Thessalonica and Berea (Acts 16:1; 17:14). Paul so trusted Timothy that he left him in Ephesus to continue combatting the error that had infiltrated the church and sent him to the church in Thessalonica to build up and encourage them (1 Thessalonians 3:2).

"To the saints and faithful brothers in Christ at Colossae"—I love how even in Paul's greeting, he is showing love and appreciation for his brothers and sisters in Christ, encouraging them from the start of the letter and reminding them of who they are in Christ. Some use the word *saint* to refer to a special honor designated to someone, but Paul uses it to refer to all believers, all those who are set apart to God. Paul also called them *faithful brothers*. As brothers (and sisters) in Christ, they were part of God's family. Paul was not picking out only a certain elite group within the church. He further calls them faithful which is a word that was used solely in the New Testament in reference to believers.

Lastly, we have a place, Colossae, which was a Roman province located in modern day Turkey. Although at one time it had been a thriving city on a main trade route between Ephesus and the Euphrates, it had diminished due to the relocation of the trade route. It was a city of both Gentiles (non-Jews) and Jews. The church here was established by Epaphras who we will learn more about later.

For Reflection: Take time first to meditate on grace and peace today and then pray the same for a few other people. Maybe you want to incorporate this into your regular prayer time when interceding for others. You can add to your list over time, you can rotate those on your list or perhaps it will become second nature to include this aspect whenever you pray for another.

DAY 2

COLOSSIANS 1:3-5A, 8

*We always thank God, the Father of our Lord Jesus Christ,
when we pray for you, since we heard of your faith in Christ Jesus
"and of the love that you have for all the saints,
because of the hope laid up for you in heaven...and [Epaphras]
has made known to us your love in the Spirit.*

Although there are many examples I can think of as I read these verses, the people that first come to mind are our brothers and sisters in Christ at a seminary in Siguatepeque, Honduras. Our first missionary trip there was in 2013. It didn't take long to connect with the students and staff at the seminary. In my life, on any given day, my love for God and others may or may not be evident. In contrast, love overflowed from those we met in Honduras, and it didn't require speaking the same language. They love God passionately. They love others contagiously. They are eager to spend time with us, to pray for us, to serve alongside with us and to learn more about God through their studies at the seminary. I give thanks to God for their example of faith and love.

As I have gotten to know our Honduran friends more and more over our six trips, my thankfulness for them has increased. In these verses we see that Paul gave thanks (and he gave it *always* when he prayed) for the Colossians whom he had likely never met. Pause for a moment and think of how often, if ever, you have given thanks for people you don't know. Let's be honest. Sometimes it is difficult enough to be thankful for who we do know without adding people we don't.

Why could Paul be thankful for believers he had never met? First, we should start with who Paul directed his thanksgiving towards: "God, the Father of our Lord Jesus Christ." I know it is easy for me to skim through this part. Giving thanks to God is not a news flash. But there are truths to unpack here. Paul did not thank the Colossian believers for being over-achievers and stirring up their own faith and love until they hit celebrity love status. He thanked the Father who gave the gracious gift of faith to the Colossians through our Lord Jesus Christ's atoning work on the cross. This inner faith overflowed in outward love (Galatians 5:6). As always, it is God at work in us not our own works (Ephesians 2:8).

Paul includes "the Father of our Lord Jesus Christ" instead of just addressing *God* or the *Father*. Paul is affirming the deity of Christ. He is magnifying the oneness of the Father and Son. Further, in verse 8 we see the Spirit's involvement. Each Person of the Trinity is involved in the Colossian believers' faith and love.

Second, Paul was thankful for the Colossian believers' faith in Christ Jesus. As we dive deeper into Colossians, we will see that false teaching was preying on the church, teaching that went against the sufficiency of Jesus' atonement. The Colossians' faith in Christ Jesus alone stood in stark contrast to the false teaching, so much so that Paul said that he and his companions had heard of their faith. It was a faith worth commending. Many may have faith, but the object of their faith is the key.

Third, Paul was thankful for the Colossian believers' love that Epaphras specifically made mention of to Paul. Although the believers in Colossae would not have had 1 Corinthians 13 to read as we can, I imagine their love, which was being extoled, exhibited much of Paul's instructions to the Corinthian believers on how to love others. It was visible love. It was action love.

What is amazing to me about the Colossians' love was that it was for *all* the saints. This is where I start getting those red grading marks on my love test. There are people around us who are easy to love—ones who give me hugs each Sunday, tell me how cute my shoes are, are full of joy, serve selflessly or bake delightful desserts. Truthfully, I wouldn't score 100% on loving these ones either, but the red pen starts losing ink when it comes to those that I don't deem so lovable. I can reserve my acts of love from them. I can cause hurt and division because I don't love *all* the saints. At best, I might get an overall C on my love test (although probably lower).

Both my lack of love and this next part bring tears to my eyes as I write. "Thank You, Father, for Jesus, for His perfect record of loving others." God isn't sitting up in heaven with His red grading pen lowering my grade at each encounter with another person. He's given me (and you) Jesus' 100%. Not only that, He is also our loving Father, we are joint-heirs with Jesus, and we are privileged to share in all the benefits of sonship.

The Colossians loved well because of the hope that was laid up for them in heaven. It is the hope of eternity with God where we will be totally complete in Christ. We will love all the saints with God's kind of love all the time. Hope spurs us to love. Hope is inextricably intertwined with faith. Paul's use of the intensive verb "laid up" indicates an irrevocable action. We can be certain in our hope.

Faith, hope and love—God's grace gifts woven together.

For Reflection: Is your faith in Jesus evident to those around you? The Colossians' faith was evident specifically through their love. Read 1 Corinthians 13. Where have you seen the Spirit at work in how you love others? Give God thanks for that work in you. Spend time in prayer for the aspects of love you need to continue to grow in, being thankful for Jesus' perfect record of loving others. (Katie Orr's devotional *Everyday Love*[2] is a wonderful in-depth study on growing in our love for others.)

Send snail mail, an email or even a text to someone you are thankful to God for the faith and love He has worked in their life that has been an encouragement to you.

For additional reading on faith, see Hebrews 10-12.

DAY 3

COLOSSIANS 1:5B-7

Of this you have heard before in the word of the truth,
the gospel, which has come to you, as indeed in the whole world
it is bearing fruit and growing—as it also does among you,
since the day you heard it and understood the grace of God in truth,
just as you learned it from Epaphras our beloved fellow servant.
He is a faithful minister of Christ on your behalf.

It was Christmas 1974. I was four years old. I was helping my Mom set up the nativity. I don't remember if I asked or if my Mom just explained the story of Jesus' birth while we placed the figures in the stable. I do know that my Mom faithfully told me the gospel that day. Especially throughout my adult years in the different places we have lived, I am thankful for several pastors who have been faithful in preaching the gospel. My life has been forever changed because of my Mom and others who faithfully taught the gospel of Christ to me.

The Gospel is the best news ever. Ever! It is the life-giving truth that Jesus, the Son of God, was born of a virgin, lived a perfect, sinless life, and then "that Christ died for our sins in accordance with the Scriptures, that He was buried, that He was raised on the third day in accordance with the Scriptures" (1 Corinthians 15:3-4). Jesus came to redeem us from our sin and restore us to right relationship with God. It is the central theme throughout Scripture. There is no other gospel (Galatians 1:8). There is no adding to it or taking from it. And the simple yet difficult thing is that we are called to just receive this priceless gift from God. We are to have faith in it, but this also is a gift from God (Ephesians 2:8-9).

Often, we limit the Gospel to our salvation and then put it away on a shelf. But did you catch how Paul described the Gospel? He said, "it is bearing fruit and growing." *Fruit* refers to the saving result of the gospel, but it is also growing. I need to remember the Gospel message every day because every day I still sin—usually multiple times in my thoughts, attitudes, words or actions. I need God's forgiveness, grace and Christ's perfect record. The Gospel's purpose is for our sanctification as well as our salvation. The continued work of the Gospel in our lives is what results in our spiritual growth, our conformity to the image of Christ. It is what encourages us through thankfulness and love for God to walk in obedience.

Paul witnessed from his own travels and from word-of-mouth that the Gospel was bearing fruit and growing in *the whole world*. Part of the false teaching at this time pronounced that special, deeper knowledge was for only a select group. In contrast, the Gospel is for the whole world. It is for all ethnicities, geographic locations, cultures and political peoples. It is a seed that can be planted anywhere and still grow and be fruitful.

Douglas J. Moo writes, "The gospel is authenticated not by its truth only nor by its power in people's lives only but by both working in tandem."[3] Truth and transformation working in tandem is what Paul sees happening in the whole world.

Paul then personalizes the Gospel. He states that it has borne fruit and has grown in the Colossian believers since the day they heard and understood God's grace. As a youth leader, although I'm sure parents and other teachers can relate, sometimes it seems like we teach, we say things over and over, and there is little or no response. Sometimes it takes a while for things to sink in, but what a blessing to see when understanding takes root and grows. The Colossian believers hadn't stopped growing since they heard and understood. No wonder Paul was thankful for God's saving and sanctifying work in their lives.

"But how are they to call on Him in whom they have not believed? And how are they to believe in Him of whom they have never heard? And how are they to hear without someone preaching?" (Romans 10:14). The Colossian church was blessed with Epaphras who was faithful to share the Gospel with them.

We know Epaphras was a fellow servant with Paul, he was willing to suffer with Paul in prison (Philemon 23), that he preached the true Gospel that resulted in fruit and growth. He was likely from the area of Colossae, and he labored in prayer for the Colossian believers (4:12). He also traveled to see Paul to get advice in combatting the heresy (false teaching) that was trying to infiltrate the church (Paul's main purpose in writing this letter). Although we know little about Epaphras, we can still perceive that he was a man passionate for God and fervent about seeing others come to saving faith and grow in sanctification.

Although a faithful minister, Epaphras was human. He didn't pitch a perfect game every time. Likewise, I know my focus in ministry is not always where it should be. In Paul David Tripp's book Awe, he has written a chapter on ministry in relation to the awe of God. "It is humbling to admit, but I have had to face the fact that the greatest danger to my ministry is me! The risk is that familiarity would cause me to lose my awe. Familiarity with God's glory is a wonderful gift of grace. To be called by God to stand up close to, think about, and communicate the elements of that glory to others is a privilege beyond expression. But it is also a very dangerous thing because I very quickly replace any vacuum of awe of God in my heart with awe of myself."[4] Epaphras was focused on God, His glory and leading the Colossian church in the same.

Tripp continues, "You will be obsessed not by how much people respect you, but by how much they worship their Redeemer."[5]

For Reflection: How would you describe your current spiritual growth? Stunted? Slow? Thriving? Wherever you are, it is always beneficial to go back to the Gospel. Remember your first love. Be in awe of the One who saved you and is sanctifying you. Remember specific times where God has brought growth and thank Him for it.

Who has been a faithful Epaphras in your life? Take some time to pray for them and their ministry. Then send them snail mail, an email or text and thank them.

DAY 4

COLOSSIANS 1:9

*And so, from the day we heard, we have not ceased
to pray for you, asking that you may be filled with the knowledge
of His will in all spiritual wisdom and understanding...*

The only prayer I clearly remember as a child is when I was about five years old. I asked God for a magic wand. I laid in bed one night and very earnestly prayed for the magic wand to be on the bed by morning. I'm sure it seemed crucial at the time as a way of getting rid of Jaws (who I was confident was lurking in the deep end of our pool) or maybe to zap a new toy into existence. In case you are wondering, the wand was nowhere to be found when I woke up. As I grew, I'm not sure that the content of my prayers changed dramatically, the specifics, yes, but not the general content. The supplication (asking God for things) part of my prayer dominated my conversations with God whether it was to pass my physics test, Grandpa to get well or a raise at my job.

Paul's prayer that goes through verse 14 was one of the passages that altered my thinking about prayer. It is one that I pray for others, and one that I treasure when someone prays through it for me. God wants us to bring all our requests to Him, but here Paul sets a pattern for praying for the most important things, spiritual things, eternal things that impact every other aspect of our lives.

We will address the rest of the prayer over the next two days, but in today's passage Paul's prayer could be summarized as being grounded in God's Word, so we will then live a life that fully glorifies God. I've found that as I continue to become more grounded in the Word, then I bring requests to God that are rooted in God's revealed will in Scripture. I am more likely to keep in mind the eternal perspective regarding the request, and I recognize Who I am bringing the request to.

Some of you may be content with the above summary of these two verses, but I was one of those who loved sentence diagramming in English and still loves to dissect Scripture to get all the treasures out of it. Ready to dig in? Let's start at the beginning, "And so..." Paul is referring back to verse 6 and the fact that the Colossians had come to saving faith. Because the Colossians have come to saving faith, Paul has specific, important intercession to make for them. And just as Paul *always* thanked God for the Colossian believers (1:3), he has not *ceased* to intercede for them.

Paul wants the Colossians to be *filled...* The idea is to complete or fully equip. In New Testament times the term was used to describe a ship completely ready for a voyage. The knowledge, wisdom and understanding Paul requested affects every part of a believer's life. They need to be completely filled and equipped to be able to "walk in a manner worthy of the Lord." Partial won't do. Paul knows to

Whom he is praying—the God of all wisdom and knowledge who delights to fully equip us. The false teachers of the time boasted that they had the fullness of truth. Paul said that Epaphras had already brought them the "word of truth." The Colossians didn't need to look elsewhere. They didn't need a new experience or secret knowledge. They needed to grow in what they already had.

Another interesting meaning of *filled* or *plēroō* is in Ephesians 5:18 where it indicates being controlled by the Spirit. My life would look different if I was controlled by God's Word and the Spirit all the time. That is exactly what Paul is asking and what he desires for the Colossians. He wants radically changed lives (vs 10). We do take into account that the Spirit's control is God's method and timing and is a very gradual process not reaching completion here on earth.

What do the Colossians (and we) need to be filled with to be equipped? Knowledge of God's will. "The *general* will of God for all His children is given clearly in the Bible. The *specific* will of God for any given situation must always agree with what He has already revealed in His Word. The better we know God's general will, the easier it will be to determine His specific guidance in daily life. Paul did not encourage the Colossians to seek visions or wait for voices. He prayed that they might get deeper into God's Word and thus have greater wisdom and insight concerning God's will."[6]

In 1 Thessalonians 4:3 God's will is our sanctification which covers a huge gamut. In 1 Thessalonians 5:18 God's will is for us to rejoice always, pray without ceasing and give thanks in all circumstances. In 1 Peter 2:12 & 15 His will is for us to be subject to government for the Lord's sake and to silence foolish people. These are just a few examples of God's will for our lives, but from these verses we can see that knowledge of God's will is always connected to obedience and action. Although we have a responsibility to act on our knowledge of God's will, we can be thankful that God has given us everything we need to know and understand His will—His Word and His Spirit (1 Corinthians 2:12).

Paul further prays for the Colossians to be "filled with the knowledge of His will *in all spiritual wisdom and understanding." All* connects back to our understanding of *filled.* Paul is not asking for the Colossians to be omniscient, to know and understand everything. He is asking that they have all the wisdom and understanding necessary for walking in a manner pleasing to God. We know from 2 Peter 1:3 that God through His divine power gives us all we need for life and godliness through the knowledge of Jesus.

Paul characterizes the wisdom by the word *spiritual.* True wisdom comes only from God. In the Old Testament are several ties between God equipping/filling and the Spirit by which He does it (Exodus 31:3; 35:31, 35; Deuteronomy 34:9; Isaiah 11:2). Wisdom isn't simply knowing what Scripture says but what it means. Wisdom organizes principles so we can apply them. It meditates on the truths we know. *Understanding* moves the knowledge and wisdom of Scripture to application in our lives. It is by the knowledge of God's will in all spiritual wisdom and understanding by the power of the Holy Spirit that we will be filled, complete.

As we wrap up today, we note that Paul prays in a certain order for a reason. Peter T. O'Brien explains, "It has been indicated that apart from the activity of God on their behalf, filling them with true discernment, they would not know as they ought to, nor grasp what he had to say in the following sections of the epistle. The prayer for knowledge *precedes* the exposition of Christ's lordship in creation and redemption (1:15-20), its ramifications (1:21-23) and the detailed interaction with the 'philosophy' of false teachers (2:6-23)."[7]

For Reflection: I know at different times I neglect studying God's Word and will. Other times I am weak in applying my knowledge. Then there are the days when I am trying to do it on my own instead of relying on the Spirit. Where are you struggling right now? First, be thankful that we have the Holy Spirit who does equip us, and Jesus' perfect record given to us of knowing, understanding and doing the will of God. Second, write down an initial step to take. Tell a friend. Have them pray for you and encourage you.

DAY 5

COLOSSIANS 1:10

So as to walk in a manner worthy of the Lord,
fully pleasing to Him, bearing fruit in every good work
and increasing in the knowledge of God.

I am a doer. A check-it-off-the-list person. A worker. It is easy for me to skim through verse 9 and focus on verse 10. "Finally! Something I can get busy doing." But we can't apply verse 10 correctly if we don't remember verse 9 (feel free to read back through yesterday's devotion). Do you remember how we ended with the quote from Peter T. O'Brien? We wouldn't be able to walk in a manner worthy of the Lord or understand anything else Paul writes in this letter apart from God actively working in us first. So, as we approach verse 10 today, we remember with gratitude that God is the one who has equipped us to walk worthily (Philippians 2:12-13). Jesus accomplished the worthy walk with perfection and has given us His record for the times we fail (imputed righteousness).

Now that we have the right foundation and motivation, let's see what Paul is calling us to. We have been blessed and equipped with knowledge of God's will for the purpose of walking worthily to the glory of God. The false teachers did not connect their knowledge to how they lived, but for believers, there is no separation. We have our responsibility in walking in obedience and working out our own sanctification motivated by our awe of God while at the same time God is equipping us by willing and working in us.

The very nature of walking implies that there is progression; there is movement. The knowledge, wisdom and understanding God gives us isn't for standing still or parking ourselves for a spiritual vacation. It is for growth. It is for conforming us to the image of Christ. At times the growth might be barely noticeable. Other times, like my tomatoes are right now, our growth seems to overflow our pot.

Our walk is to be in "a manner worthy of the Lord, fully pleasing to Him…" Being worthy of the Lord or fully pleasing to Him is to satisfy God in all respects. Daunting? Seem impossible? This is why we hold on to the context. If this command was just up to us to do the work, we would fail regularly. However, we fall back on our loving Father who has equipped us with the Holy Spirit who is always working in us with the same power that raised Jesus from the dead (verse 11; Romans 8:10-11), who has given us knowledge, wisdom and understanding (verse 9) so we know what to do, and who has given us Jesus' perfect record of walking worthily and always pleasing God (2 Corinthians 5:21).

A *worthy walk* is a fundamental concept, calling the believer to live in accordance with his/her identity in Christ. Paul describes in more detail what this worthy walk looks like with four participles. The first two descriptions are in verse 10. The second two, "strengthened with all power" and "giving thanks", are in verses 11 and 12.

The first characterization of a worthy walk, bearing fruit, is an echo of verse 6 where Paul expresses thanksgiving for the spread of the saving work of the Gospel. Here, in intercession, Paul shifts the meaning to the sanctifying work of the Gospel in the Colossian believers. In John 15:8 Jesus said, "By this my Father is glorified, that you bear much fruit and so prove to be my disciples." Bearing fruit is evidence of the saving work of the Gospel. The fruit of the Spirit listed in Galatians 5:22-23 will be manifested in our lives in growing measures. Bearing fruit will bring forth more disciples (2 Timothy 2:2). Bearing fruit proceeds in praise to God (Hebrews 13:15).

The fruit we bear is in *every* good work. This is not sporadic service to God when we feel like it. Charles Spurgeon argues, "Here is room and range enough—in 'every good work.' Have you the ability to preach the gospel? Preach it! Does a little child need comforting? Comfort it! Can you stand up and vindicate a glorious truth before thousands? Do it! Does a poor saint need a bit of dinner from your table? Send it to her. Let works of obedience, testimony, zeal, charity, piety, and philanthropy all be found in your life. Do not select big things as your special line, but glorify the Lord also in the littles—'fruitful in every good work.'"[8]

We again see the word *work*. It is easy to jump back to what we can do on our own, but we don't want to disengage this one word from what we know from other passages of Scripture. We know that it is God who works in us for us to be able to bear fruit in every good work. We also recognize that God created us in Christ Jesus as His workmanship to do the good works which were prepared beforehand, for us to walk in them (Ephesians 2:10). More reminders that this is not our own solo effort. It is a result of what God has already done and is doing in and for us primarily through the ordinary, every-day things because this is where most of our lives are lived.

Second, Paul describes a worthy walk as "increasing in the knowledge of God." The Colossian believers had heard and received the word of truth. Paul has prayed for them to be filled with knowledge of the will of God in all spiritual wisdom and understanding, but this is not a one-time event. The tense of the verbs in the original Greek indicates a progression. "It is probably right to conclude that the Colossian Christians would receive further knowledge as they were obedient to the knowledge of God they had already received."[9]

Peter instructs believers to "grow in the grace and knowledge of our Lord and Savior Jesus Christ" (2 Peter 3:18). God continues to sanctify and grow us until we reach completion on the day of Jesus Christ (Philippians 1:6). It is this wonderful, continuous circle of knowing God, growing as we walk in obedience, knowing God more through our obedience, growing more in our knowledge of God, etc., until we are complete.

For Reflection: How would you classify your "good works"? Are you doing them in your own strength? Are you leaving it all up to God or are you balanced between what God calls you to do and relying and being motivated by what He has done and is doing?

What is hindering fruit in your life (Hebrews 12:1)? Is there sin to repent of? Are there activities or entertainment that sets you on a detour? Do you need to be more purposeful in personal time with God? Is there a specific fruit of the Spirit that might need intentional cultivating? "Great grace is needed—but great grace is provided!"[10]

DAY 6

COLOSSIANS 1:11-14

*May you be strengthened with all power according
to His glorious might, for all endurance and patience with joy,
giving thanks to the Father, who has qualified you to share in the
inheritance of the saints in light. He has delivered us from the domain
of darkness and transferred us to the kingdom of His beloved Son,
in whom we have redemption, the forgiveness of sins.*

Remember the story of Cinderella? Poor girl enslaved by her mean step-mother and step-sisters. Dressed in rags. No hope for her future until the ball. In a single night her life is changed forever. In the end, the prince rescues her and takes her to his kingdom to live happily ever after. Yes, yes, a nice fairy tale. In our verses today we read of something even more magnificent because it is true. We were in a far worse place than Cinderella, but the King, God the Father, transferred us to the kingdom of His beloved Son for all eternity. By the blood of His own Son, He redeemed us, forgave our sins, made us joint-heirs with His Son, made us His children and will bring us to Himself for eternity. No fairy tale!

When I read about endurance and patience with joy and ponder some of my circumstances, I think, "You've got to be kidding. I may squeak through this, but God, you want me to be joyful too?" I'm so grateful that once again God is not calling us to a task for which He doesn't equip us. Paul himself went through incredible sufferings (2 Corinthians 11:16-33), but we see that even in prison he praised God (Acts 16:25). Joy is his theme throughout his letter to the Philippians. So, when Paul writes about endurance and patience with joy, he writes from experience. He writes knowing Who the source is.

In verses 9 and 10, Paul has begun praying asking God that the Colossian believers would be growing in their knowledge of His will and that this knowledge would lead them to walk worthily of the Lord. Paul didn't leave it at that. He knew they would need Supernatural help, so he continues his prayer with a request that they "be strengthened with all power according to His glorious might." As we saw before, we need help and God has given us His Holy Spirit to empower us.

As so often we see with God, He abundantly provides for us. Paul uses three synonyms to emphasize his point. One word won't suffice. First, the word *strengthened* is the Greek word *dynamoō*. Does it look vaguely familiar? We get our English word *dynamite* from it. It describes an inherent power similar to everything bundled up inside the cardboard wrapper of dynamite that causes the huge explosion. It is strength that enables us from the inside.

The second word *power* is similar to *strengthened*. The Greek is *dynamis*. The King James translates it as *might*. It has a broader meaning than inherent power alone. It is often associated with miraculous power or force.

The third word is *might* which the King James translates as power (you can see why they are all synonymous). The Greek for it is *kratos*. It can include the idea of dominion. Paul says "His glorious might" which even further describes the power he is praying to enable us. It is God's very own power. I don't know about you, but that blows my mind. What an amazing, faithful, generous Father we have to equip us so incredibly. Does "endurance and patience with joy" seem possible now?

Now that we know how amazingly God has equipped us, let's look a little closer at what we are equipped for. Endurance is tied to difficult circumstances. We all experience trials at one time or another. For some it is the death of a loved one or a battle with cancer, chronic pain or dementia. For others it is the loss or stress of a job, a spouse addicted to pornography or a child who has turned away from their family and faith. Perhaps it is the darkness of depression or abuse. How do we endure often through trial upon trial? Dr. V. Raymond Edman, late Wheaton College President said, "It is always too soon to quit." We persevere despite the circumstances. We persevere because we are strengthened by the very power of God that we just discussed. We hold to that truth even when our circumstances seem overwhelming.

Paul also prayed that we would be equipped for patience. Patience focuses on enduring problematic people. We all have those in our lives too. It means we exercise self-restraint. We do not seek revenge. We know we have experienced God's long-suffering towards us (2 Peter 3:9), so we can extend that to others. It is a fruit of the Spirit (Galatians 5:22), so we know that it isn't a gift some possess, and others don't. We also know that it is something we deliberately put on as children chosen by God (Colossians 3:12).

Both endurance and patience are qualified by the words *all* (there is no circumstance or person that is exempt from us enduring and being patient) and by *joy*. Unlike happiness, joy is independent of circumstances and people. It is rooted in God, what He has done and our identity in Him. It is a fruit of the Spirit, so it is another non-negotiable (oh, how we like to pick and choose our fruit of the Spirit, don't we?).

Paul goes on to pray that we give thanks to the Father. We've just seen how mightily He has equipped us. Remember the beginning of today's devotion and our not-a-fairy tale? That is even more reason to give thanks. The Greek word is *eucharisteō*. I am far from being a Greek scholar, but from the little I have studied, this has been one of my favorite words. On Day 1 we talked about it from Paul's greeting. It is a verb meaning "to be grateful or to give thanks." It contains the word *charis* (grace). *Chara*, another derivative, means joy. Here in verses 11 and 12 we have a swirl of joy and thankfulness in light of God's gift of grace specifically in His strength and inheritance that He gives us through redemption in Jesus.

If thankfulness is what we are "putting on", complaining is what we are "putting off". Paul David Tripp explains, "If praise is celebrating God's awesome glory, then complaint is anti-praise. Not only does complaint fail to recognize His grandeur, it questions His power and character. If you believe that God is the Creator and controller of all that is, then it is impossible to complain about your circumstances without complaining about God...And if our contentment rests on life being easy, comfortable and pleasurable, we'll have no contentment this side of eternity [in a fallen world]. Only when the awe of God rules your heart will you be able to have joy even when people disappoint you and life gets hard. Awe means your heart will be filled more with a sense of blessing than with a sense of want. You will be daily blown away by what you have been given rather than being constantly disturbed by what you think you need. Awe produces gratitude, gratitude instills joy, and the harvest of joy is contentment."[11]

It is important to note that we are not just thankful for the inheritance we receive, but we are thankful that God qualified us for it. It is His gift to us. On our own, we would never be qualified to receive it. We would be qualified only for God's wrath. *Hikanoō* was used for an athlete who qualified to compete. Through Christ's finished work on the cross, God qualifies or makes us sufficient to receive our inheritance.

Paul ends his prayer with a declaration of our status—a reminder of what God has done for us and an encouragement of who we are in Christ. God rescued us from danger, from Satan's domain. He then transfers us to His Son's eternal kingdom. Transfer loses some of its meaning in our English and without the context of Paul's time. When a ruler conquered a people, he would transfer defeated people back to his kingdom. In Christ, we are transferred as victors. Although we may still struggle with the sin belonging to the domain of darkness, Jesus broke the power of Satan over us. Satan no longer has rights to us. Jesus redeemed us by meeting the holy demands of God's law through His death and resurrection. In Him we are forgiven. Jesus cancelled all our debt so we will never be under the domain of darkness again. This right here is our powerful motivation for walking worthily. Amen!

For Reflection: A couple years ago I read Ann Voskamp's *One Thousand Gifts Devotional*[12]. She had been challenged to write, over time, one thousand things she was thankful for. It made her, and me in reading her book, learn to look for all the little gifts of grace God has lavished on us every day. I am almost to one thousand in my journal. It has transformed my thinking to be more grateful throughout the day. Today, start your own thankful journal. You can start with things from today's verses, but that is just the tip of the iceberg. Keep going. Pray for eyes that see and search out God's gifts of grace that are all around.

DAY 7

COLOSSIANS 1:15-16

He is the image of the invisible God, the firstborn of all creation.
For by Him all things were created in heaven and on earth,
visible and invisible, whether thrones or dominions or rulers
or authorities—all things were created through Him and for Him.

It was in my high school Church History (or maybe Doctrine) class with Mr. Strimple that I first remember hearing about creeds and confessions. They are a regular component of some churches, but either the churches we went to when I was a younger child didn't use them or I hadn't paid attention. For those who might not be familiar, a creed is a statement of beliefs, usually religious beliefs. One of the earliest Christian creeds was "Jesus is Lord" in response to Rome's command for Christian's to publicly declare "Caesar is Lord." Easy to see the importance of even that simple creed.

In a radio interview, R.C. Sproul shared, "The great creeds of church history, such as the Nicene Creed and the Chalcedonian Creed, were written in response to serious heretical views that were arising and threatening the very essence of the Christian faith. This is true also of the historic confessions. These confessions were an attempt to crystallize the essence of doctrine found in sacred Scripture. They were never to be seen as a substitute for Scripture or as having authority over Scripture. Rather, they give a summary of what Christians believe as defined in terms of confessional orthodoxy."[13]

"But there is more. First, they remind us that we didn't start the fire. They remind us that we have stepped into a stream that precedes us—that our fathers are at this table. It puts us in our context. Second, they teach us of His glory. They are tools by which we can enter into His character, and worship. They are delights, not burdens, radiant windows as well as effective gates. Maybe our fathers were on to something. And maybe we ought to get into them."[14]

Why all this creed and confessions talk? Verses 15-20 which we study over the next three days is an early creed. Some call it a hymn, but essentially it is a creed. It is a statement of belief about the Person of Christ in response to heresy which still exists today. When I visit a new church, one of the first things I do is look for their statement of beliefs. I want to know going in what their basic beliefs are. In these verses, Paul is giving the Colossians and us a concise statement of belief about the Person of Jesus that they needed to know. It was key. Anything contradictory was heresy.

Some of the heresy around Colossae specifically questioned the Person of Christ. These heretics believed that the physical body was evil. Therefore, it was insane to them that God Himself would take on flesh. He could not be fully God and fully man. Do you see why this could be critical? Do you see why Paul was giving the

Colossian believers a concise creed? These verses more than any-where else in Scripture defend the deity of Christ, and His sufficiency in reconciling man to God.

Paul begins with describing Jesus as "the image of the invisible God". The Greek is important here. There are two Greek words that we might translate as *image*. The first, *homoioma*, refers to some-thing that is similar. Jesus is not similar to God. He is God. Paul used the word *eikon* (Ring a bell? Icon.). This is an exact copy or repre-sentation (Hebrews 1:3; John 14:9). It brings with it the idea of man-ifestation. In the case of Jesus, God's very nature and character are fully revealed or manifested in Christ. The invisible God who could not be seen in the Old Testament is seen in Jesus. In Exodus 33:18-23 when Moses asks to see God's manifested presence or glory, he is granted only a glimpse of the back. But in Jesus, the invisible (or glimpse) is visible.

The second description of Jesus in verse 15 is that He is "The firstborn of all creation." We usually think of firstborn in a chrono-logical way like a firstborn child. By this definition, Jesus would be a created being and not God. Jesus can't be created and be the Creator (verse 16). If being the first created is what Paul was con-veying, he would be agreeing with the heretics. Paul is speaking to Jesus' preeminence (supremacy) and right of inheritance over all of creation. Jesus existed before creation, and He is exalted above it.

Verse 16 starts with *For* (or because). Jesus is preeminent over creation because He is the One who did the creating. Everything that is and has ever been was created by Jesus. This phrase of "all things were created" indicates that all things stand created or remain created. "The permanence of the universe rests, then, on Christ far more than on gravity. It is a Christ-centric universe."[15]

Paul gives us a specific list that is under Jesus' rule. He covers a full range with "visible and invisible," and then he lists different authorities. Paul explicitly shows Jesus' immeasurable superiority over every being (human, angel, demon) that the false teachers might bring up particularly trust in angels. False teaching confused the limited and God-given role of angels as "ministering spirits" (Hebrews 1:14) with beings of greater power worthy of worship. So Paul's statement is another blow to their teaching.

Paul's conclusion in verse 16 is a further refutation of heresy in his use of three different prepositions—by, through and for Him. Warren Wiersbe describes this by saying, "Greek philosophers taught that everything needed a primary cause (by—Christ planned it), an instrumental cause (through—He produced it) and a final cause (for—He did it for His own pleasure)."[16] Paul is skilled in taking false thinking and language and using it to reveal God's truth.

We can be encouraged by verse 16. Because everything that is created is by, through and for Jesus, even though creation remains under the curse of sin (Romans 8:22), we can still use it for God's glory and our enjoyment (1 Timothy 6:17).

For Reflection: Think of a current circumstance you are in. How does Jesus' preeminence impact your perspective on it?

Add to your thankful journal from today's devotion. What about Jesus' preeminence are you thankful for? When you think of all Jesus created, which things do you appreciate and enjoy?

Take some time to read through some of the old creeds and confessions (The Apostles' Creed, The Nicene Creed, The Athanasian Creed, The Heidelberg Catechism, The Westminster Confession of Faith or others). Also, many of the old hymns contain mini creeds. Look for them next time one is sung in church. It is good to consider what we believe (2 Timothy 2:15).

DAY 8

COLOSSIANS 1:17-18

And He is before all things, and in Him all things hold together. And He is the head of the body, the church. He is the beginning, the firstborn from the dead, that in everything He might be preeminent.

Have you ever come home from shopping, you're in a hurry or maybe just feeling some extra strength, so you try to carry in all the bags at once? I have. Sometimes I've made it. Other times, I've realized too late that it was too much to attempt at once. Now imagine everything you possibly can in the entire world plus the zillion kabillion things you can't imagine. Jesus is holding all of that together. This is part of what we will explore today.

In verse 17 Paul points us back to verses 15 and 16 and the fact that Jesus existed and is preeminent over all creation. Remember, Jesus being "before all things" does not mean that He was *created* before everything else. We know that He is eternal. "I am the Alpha and the Omega, the first and the last, the beginning and the end" (Revelation 22:13. See also John 1:1-2; 8:58; 1 John 1:1).

Naturally, our human thinking completely revolves around time because everything as we know it in this world has a beginning and an end. This is not true of Jesus. Adam Clarke explains, "As all creation necessarily exists in *time*, and had a *commencement*, and there was an infinite duration in which it *did not exist*, whatever was *before* or *prior* to that must be *no part of creation*; and the Being who existed prior to creation, and *before all things*-all existence of every kind, must be the unoriginated and eternal God: but Paul says, *Jesus Christ was before all things*; ergo, the apostle conceived Jesus Christ to be truly, and essentially God."[17]

Next Paul declares that "in Him all things hold together." Proverbs 3:19-20 says, "The Lord by wisdom founded the earth; by understanding He established the heavens; by His knowledge the deeps broke open, and the clouds drop down the dew." These verses are evidence of God's wisdom, knowledge and understanding in creating everything from the massive foundations of the earth and the heavens to the tiniest drop of dew. The same is true for all that Jesus holds together. Currently humans have discovered the quark as the smallest particle. From the largest thing you can think of like the earth's foundations or all of the heavens which we are still discovering down to the quark, Jesus holds it all together. He sustains it; He maintains the power and precise balance necessary for all of life to exist and continue (Hebrews 1:3). Without Him, all we know would fall apart. This further affirms Jesus' deity.

In verse 18 we have a familiar analogy—Jesus as the head of the church body (Ephesians 5:23). He describes the church as a body in great detail in 1 Corinthians 12:12-31. In Ephesians 4:15 and Colossians 2:10, we read of Christ as the head. The head is the center of control for the rest of the body. It gives the body life and direction. Jesus is the head of all rule and authority.

The church is the body. Especially today with so many denominations within the church, I think this is a good reminder. The body is singular. Jesus isn't a head of many bodies. He is the head of *the* body, the church, the universal church. I understand why there are different denominations, and many of the distinctions are good, but it is also important to remember that in Jesus we are still one body. "The metaphor of the church as the body of Christ suggests an intimate union with Him and other believers. Our Savior is building a church united in faith and love, with all believers regarded as equally significant in the body."[18]

Jesus is the beginning. He is the source of everything. The church emanates from Jesus as the head of the body. He gave the church life through His propitiating death and resurrection.

He is "the firstborn from the dead." Think back with me to the time of the Israelites' slavery in Egypt before their exodus. They were to put a spotless lamb's blood on the two doorposts and the lintel of their houses. If they did this, God would pass over their house and spare their firstborn while the Egyptians' firstborn would die (Exodus 12). This is a picture of what Jesus would do. It was not the righteousness of the Israelites compared to the Egyptians that spared them or our righteousness that spares us. The Israelites' firstborn were saved and we are saved because of the substitutionary death of another. Isaiah 53 describes the future Lamb that would once and for all redeem us. Paul avows that Jesus is the fulfillment of Isaiah 53 by calling Him the firstborn. But unlike the Israelites in Egypt, Jesus was not spared. He was the required, fully human, only perfect substitution.

That Jesus is "the firstborn from the dead" also give us hope because it is assurance of our future. We can have confidence in our future resurrection. Jesus conquered death for us. Therefore, He is preeminent over everything, including death which had been subject to the curse resulting from the fall. Jesus said in John 11:25-26 that He is the resurrection and the life. In the crucifixion, Satan thought he had the victory, but through His resurrection Jesus proved that He was preeminent even over the grave. Hallelujah!

For Reflection: Jesus not only holds all things together like gravity, but He also holds together every bit pertaining to your individual life. Luke 12:7 says that God has even the hairs on your head numbered. How does Jesus holding all the details of your life together (or every created thing) encourage you specifically? I know that all too often I try to hold things together in my life, in my strength. I try to control things instead of trusting them to the One who holds all things together. I still need to respond in obedience to what God calls me to, but part of obedience is trusting God. Where are you trying to hold it all together? How will you choose to trust God in obedience in that situation? Outline specific steps. Write out applicable verses to remind you.

How does remembering that Jesus is the head of the church affect your daily living? Are you looking to Him for daily direction? Are you looking at your brothers and sisters in Christ in light of the unity you share as the body of Christ? Is there something you can do today, this week to seek unity under the headship of Jesus?

DAY 9

COLOSSIANS 1:19-20

*For in Him all the fullness of God was pleased to dwell,
and through Him to reconcile to Himself all things, whether on earth
or in heaven, making peace by the blood of His cross.*

I recently got a bracelet with Romans 5:8 on it, my "favoritest" verse (I have several favorites). "but God shows His love for us in that while we were still sinners, Christ died for us." It's my reminder that there was nothing within me to reconcile myself to God. In fact, in Romans 5:10 Paul goes beyond calling us just sinners. He says we were enemies of God. Enemies don't make reconciliation and bring peace. Colossians 1:21 says that we were hostile in mind. It is Jesus alone that brought reconciliation and peace between God and man through His blood on the cross.

Lauren Daigle's song *How Can It Be*[19] speaks to the same idea.

You plead my cause

You right my wrongs

You break my chains

You overcome

You gave Your life

To give me mine

You say that I am free

How can it be? How can it be?

Though I fall, You can make me new

From this death I will rise with You

Oh the grace reaching out for me

How can it be? Did you notice all the times Lauren Daigle says, "You"? It is only by the grace of God at work through the death and resurrection of Jesus. He pleads our cause before the Father, a continuous testimony that His finished work covers our sin. He rights our wrongs in that we not only have forgiveness and payment for our sins, but we have been given Christ's righteousness. He breaks our chains because sin no longer has control over us. We, by the Spirit, can now choose obedience. All this is because Jesus gave His life for us to live and be reconciled to God.

If you are not sure of the deity of Christ, verse 19 makes it abundantly clear. Paul is deliberate in the words he chooses. Remember that Paul is responding to circulating heresy. The false teachers believed that divine attributes were *divided* among various created beings. Paul's use of "all the fullness" pokes at the false teachers. Contrary to their teaching Paul says that all of the fullness of God dwelt completely in One being alone, Jesus. No part of the Father's character, attributes or essence was lacking in Jesus.

Charles Spurgeon instructs, "Two mighty words: 'fullness' a substantial, comprehensive, expressive word in itself, and 'all,' a great little word including everything. When combined in the expression, 'all fullness,' we have before us a superlative wealth of meaning."[20]

"In Christ, all of God's attributes are manifested and glorified. Natural theology may give a person a dim knowledge of God's attributes, but in Christ, these attributes 'sparkle' because they are revealed in redemption. Some even call Christ the 'stage' on which God displays His attributes in their harmony for the world to witness."[21] Mark Jones goes on to illustrate in one example how each of God's attributes were shown in Jesus' atonement for our sin.

Jesus' deity in conjunction with His full humanity made possible His victory in reconciliation. *Reconcile* in the Greek was to exchange. In reconciling us, Jesus exchanged or restored our broken relationship with God to a right relationship through His blood. This reconciliation extends to "all things, whether on earth or in heaven." Romans 8:18-23 reminds us that all creation was affected by sin and is awaiting the restoration made possible through Jesus' blood.

It is only by the blood of His cross that reconciliation and peace are possible. Jesus' death on our behalf, not any effort of our own, reconciles us to God. Praise God for His grace that brings us peace.

There are many thoughts to wade through on what all is included in the reconciliation and the making of peace. We do know at some point that there will be a new heaven and a new earth (Revelation 21:1). We know that willingly or not "every knee should bow, in heaven and on earth and under the earth, and every tongue confess that Jesus Christ is Lord, to the glory of God the Father" (Philippians 2:10-11). But our focus is on the reconciliation of believers to God as continued in verses 21-22.

If we look at verses 15-20 as a hymn or a creed, verses 19 and 20 are the peak, the point the preceding verses are building towards. What a peak indeed!

For Reflection: These verses give us plenty to both adore God and thank Him for. In Jesus, we see the fullness of God. We can know the Father through what we know of the Son. We behold God's attributes and character. What in Jesus do you adore or leaves you in awe?

We are forever reconciled to God in Christ. Nothing will ever separate us from Him (Romans 8:31-39). What aspect of our reconciliation makes you most thankful today? No more condemnation, eternity with God, restored fellowship, etc.?

DAY 10

COLOSSIANS 1:21-22

And you, who once were alienated and hostile in mind,
doing evil deeds, He has now reconciled in
His body of flesh by His death, in order to present you holy and
blameless and above reproach before Him.

As a Christian I have continued to sin. There are some things I look back on and wonder how I could be saved and still say or do something like that. There are times I have simmered with anger. Times I have said incredibly unkind things about or to someone. Times I have lied. Times I have not loved my husband well. In Jerry Bridges' book *Respectable Sins*, he details many of the sins we tend to dismiss lightly or justify such as anxiety, discontentment, pride, ungratefulness, selfishness, lack of self-control, impatience, irritability, anger, judgmentalism, envy, sins of the tongue and worldliness.

Pretty sure I'm guilty of all those and more even as one who has come to saving faith.

But what about before I was covered by Jesus' work on the cross? Paul says I (and you) "were alienated and hostile in mind, doing evil deeds." I don't know about you, but I am grateful for the word *were*. I'm thankful for verse 22 and to know that Jesus reconciled me to present me holy and blameless and above reproach even though I continue to sin. It should bring me to my knees in awe and wonder. Holy and blameless and above reproach before Him. That is radical transformation.

Have you ever known an unsaved person who seemed nice or did "good" things? It can be hard to think of someone like that being hostile towards God or doing evil things. But Paul describes all of us in this way as well as alienated. No one is merely neutral towards God. Paul paints a grim picture.

We were alienated. We were completely cut off from God. Have you ever been alone? Our alienation was as spiritually alone as you can get. We were hostile in mind. The King James translates it as being enemies of God. We were hateful towards God in our minds even if it wasn't visible to others. One commentator said that this hostility in our minds is evident by our unrepentant sin. Lastly, we were characterized by our evil deeds. Our wicked acts were a result of our alienation and hostile minds. *Hostile in mind* and *doing evil deeds* shows that both our minds and our wills work together in rebelling against God. Romans 1:18-32 and 3:9-20 also depict our abominable and hopeless condition before the Holy Spirit in grace drew us to Jesus.

Can you begin to glimpse the amazing love of God to redeem us from this (Romans 5:6-8)? By His death, Jesus redeems us from being alienated, hateful enemies to being holy, blameless and above reproach. In His one perfect, beautiful, atoning act on the cross, He changed our status forever.

You may wonder why Paul didn't just say it was by Jesus' death that our status change was made possible. Why do we need to know it was "in His body of flesh?" Body and flesh are redundant, aren't they? There are at least two purposes in Paul's choice of words. First, it reminds us of Jesus' humanity. He was a real man, fully human. Don't think for a nanosecond that His deity overrode one ounce of the physical, emotional or spiritual pain He endured leading up to or on the cross. He was just as human as you or me, yet without sin.

Second, Paul again was attacking the false teaching. On Day 7 we learned that the false teachers believed the physical body was evil. Paul was emphasizing that it was in Jesus' physical body that He died and was resurrected.

Paul's next words "in order" give us the purpose of Jesus' death and our reconciliation: personal holiness. Holy refers to our new positional relationship with God. He freed us from sin's power and set us apart to Himself. This is only possible because of Jesus' righteousness being imputed to us. Jesus' perfect, righteous record is now ours. This is how Jesus "presents" us holy, blameless and without reproach. We have been justified—just as if I'd never sinned and just as if I'd always obeyed (2 Corinthians 5:21).

We are presented blameless (again only possible by Jesus' imputed righteousness). This is an Old Testament picture of the sacrifices that were required to be without any blemish to be acceptable. Can you imagine that? God sees us without even one blemish or speck (sin) because of Christ. We are presented above reproach. In Romans 8:1 Paul writes, "There is therefore now no condemnation for those who are in Christ Jesus." Later in Romans 8:31-34 he says that if God is for us, who can be against us? No one can bring a charge against us because God has justified us. No one can condemn us because of Jesus' death, resurrection and ascension where He now intercedes for us. We tend to think of Jesus' intercession as only praying for us, but in Romans 8 the picture is that Jesus is the visible reminder (intercession) to the Father that He took the penalty of our sin and gave us His righteousness. He is advocating or interceding for us.

For reflection: How does knowing your condition before you came to saving faith impact your perspective of God's love for you?

How does your justified status before God motivate you? Are there things to add to your thankful journal if you started one or to spend time in grateful prayer for?

DAY 11

COLOSSIANS 1:23

If indeed you continue in the faith, stable
and steadfast, not shifting from the hope of the gospel that you
heard, which has been proclaimed in all creation under heaven,
and of which I, Paul, became a minister.

As a young girl I loved to ice-skate. Remaining stable and not
sliding around uncontrollably was crucial to staying off my tail end.
Of course, ice is slippery. It is easy to slide around and fall if you don't
know what you are doing or if your blades are dull. I took lessons.
I practiced what I was taught. I grew in my abilities. I wasn't an ice-
skater just because I said so or owned skates and an ice-skating dress.
Someone could come to the rink and see evidence (although often
feeble) of my claim to be an ice-skater.

In verse 22 Paul stated that Jesus reconciled us by His death.
It has been completed, so why does verse 23 begin with *if*? In the

English language, *if* tends to be a word that expresses doubt or a required condition. It has caused much debate over what Paul means.

Other ways it can be translated that might be closer to the original Greek meaning is *since, in as much* or *seeing that.* In verse 22 we know that Paul is addressing believers because he is describing those who *were* alienated and hostile in mind (verse 21) but are now reconciled to God through Jesus. So, we would read verse 23 as evidence of a reconciled person by four qualifications: continuing in the faith, stable, steadfast and not shifting from the hope of the gospel. Jesus talked about good trees bearing good fruit (Matthew 7:17-18). James 2:14-26 reiterates that true faith is evidenced by works. Verse 23 is some of that good fruit. I'm sure we all know of someone who walked the aisle and professed their faith in God or a small child who did, but as the years go on, there is never any evidence of a changed life. Paul says one indication of a changed life is a person who continues on in the faith they professed.

As a new creation in Christ (2 Corinthians 5:17), we will persevere in our faith and be sanctified by the Spirit's work in us. Even true believers will have downs as well as ups. We don't quit sinning the second we come to saving faith, but our general direction is continued conformity to the image of Jesus. Think of Peter or David. They committed some big sins, but they weren't eternally lost. The Holy Spirit continued sanctifying them. We have God's promise that He will complete the work He began in us (Philippians 1:6). The fact that Jesus reconciled us, and that God transferred us from the domain of darkness to Jesus' kingdom is incredible motivation to persevere with gratitude.

R.C. Sproul used the term "preservation of the saints" instead of perseverance of the saints to put the emphasis where it rightly belongs, on God. Ultimately that we are kept until eternity is completely by the power and grace of God. This may be a new concept for some or maybe something you haven't thought about. Jesus said, "And this is the will of Him who sent Me, that I should lose nothing of all that He has given Me, but raise it up on the last day" (John 6:39-40). In John 10:27-29 Jesus said that no one could snatch His sheep from His hand. Paul wrote in Romans 8:35-39 that there is nothing in all of creation that can ever separate us from His love. In Ephesians 1:13-14 Paul assures us that the Holy Spirit is the guarantee of our inheritance until we are actually in heaven. Hebrews 7:25; 10:14 and 1 Peter 1:3-5 also comfort us with the assurance of salvation.

The evidence of a reconciled person is that they are stable, steadfast and unshifting. The region in which Colossae was located was known for earthquakes. Those in the Colossian church would know what it was like for things to fall off shelves, slide around or even struggle themselves to keep their footing. Paul used words that were equated with a building's firm foundation. This reminds me of the parable Jesus told about the wise and foolish builders (Matthew 7:24-27; Luke 6:46-49). Jesus compares the wise man who built his house on the rock to one who hears His words and obeys. That house will withstand the storms—stable, steadfast, not shifting. He has a solid foundation.

That Gospel is that foundation (we discussed the Gospel in detail on Day 3). The message of the Gospel gives us hope. Because of Jesus' death and resurrection, our hope as Christians is that Jesus will return for us (Titus 2:13; Colossians 1:5). This is the good news that the Colossian believers had heard. It was the good news that was proclaimed in all the earth. It was the good news that Paul proclaimed. Rome was the center of the known world at this time, so in a sense, the gospel preached through Rome was reaching all around the known world as it went out from Rome. Paul might also have been thinking of the fulfillment of the gospel going to the whole world that we see in Matthew 24:14. Either way, we know the gospel is not just for a select group of people. It is not for only certain ethnicities, genders or classes. Paul preached to Jews and Gentiles. It is for everyone and will be made known in all the world.

For Reflection: Would you describe your faith as stable, steadfast and not shifting from the hope you have in the gospel? Or is this a period of struggle? First, whether stable or shifting, remember that it is only by the Spirit that we persevere and are steadfast.

Second, no matter where you are at (in the middle of an earthquake or planted on a solid rock) keep building your foundation by time in the Word and prayer. Remind yourself of the gospel and that God will keep you through eternity.

Third, find a friend in Christ to share with. If you are on the solid rock right now, share what you've been learning about God and what has been encouraging you. It might be what someone in a current earthquake needs to get their footing. If you're the one being shifted here and there, ask for prayer. Share your need. Not only did God give us the Spirit to equip us, but He gave us each other to encourage and build one another up.

DAY 12

COLOSSIANS 1:24-27

*Now I rejoice in my sufferings for your sake, and in my flesh
I am filling up what is lacking in Christ's afflictions for the sake
of His body, that is, the church, of which I became a minister
according to the stewardship from God that was given to me for you,
to make the word of God fully known, the mystery hidden for ages
and generations but now revealed to His saints. To them God chose
to make known how great among the Gentiles are the riches of the
glory of this mystery, which is Christ in you, the hope of glory.*

Rejoicing in suffering may seem like a strange thing to do. Suffering by its own nature is far from pleasant and not a normal cause for rejoicing. A couple years ago my dermatologist found melanoma in my left eyebrow. I had to go in five different times as the doctor tried to cut it all out without taking more of my face than necessary. When it was all removed, I went through a reconstructive surgery (thankfully asleep for that). I have not experienced much other pain that was as acute as the ten minutes of numbing shots I received before each cutting away. It made me dizzy and nauseous. I'm thankful for my husband and parents who drove me home after each round. The suffering through that for the sake of the pain alone was definitely not cause for rejoicing.

However, there were two things that did cause me to rejoice in the midst of the pain. First, the melanoma did not burrow into my eye or spread anywhere internal. As melanoma can lead to death, I was definitely rejoicing. Second, and the cause for greater rejoicing, was that I was able to share the hope that I have with all my doctors. With the surgical dermatologist, I had mentioned God or church in my first two appointments, but the conversation quickly shifted. The third appointment, the doctor was really concerned about how I was doing with the repeated cutting. This time I was able to share why I was at peace and the hope that I had no matter the outcome. The pathologist who has run all my biopsies was also very concerned when this, my second round of melanoma, came back positive. My regular dermatologist was able to share my faith with him, and why I was probably the least of all patients to worry about. My understanding is that much of the pathology department was praying for me.

Let me emphasize that the only reason I was so at peace through both rounds of cancer was because of what God had worked in me. I can't take one iota of credit because I know my human tendency would have been to worry about something as serious as cancer. I know that God is sovereign. I know that He is working everything for the good of those that love Him to conform us to the image of His Son (Romans 8:28-29) and for His own glory. I know that He loves me. Although there are other areas in which I struggle, with my health God has granted me rest in what I know is true and the ability to rejoice at what He is doing. Going through the five cuttings may have been the only way my doctor would have listened to my faith, and if God can use my temporary suffering to draw my doctor to saving faith, then it is suffering worth rejoicing.

Paul endured much more than I did including his current imprisonment. His suffering was specifically because of the gospel, but no matter what he endured, he rejoiced in his suffering. The false teachers thought that Paul's suffering diminished the impact of the gospel he preached. Paul viewed it differently (Philippians 2:17). He saw the fruit in the lives of those in Colossae, Philippi and other churches. He was thankful to be counted worthy to suffer as His Savior had. Paul was other focused not self-centered—"for the sake of His body, that is, the church" (verse 24b). He wasn't suffering as an ascetic, focused on his own holiness, growth and perfection. In humility, following Jesus' example, Paul counted others as more significant than himself and put their needs above his own (Philippians 2:3-11).

The second part of verse 24 may cause some questions. What does Paul mean by saying he was filling up what was lacking in Christ's afflictions? Was Jesus' atonement somehow insufficient? Let's answer that with a resounding "No!" as it would be contrary to Paul's teachings elsewhere on the sufficiency of Jesus' sacrifice (1:15-23 and chapter 2). The Greek word for afflictions is *thlipsis*. It was never used in reference to Jesus' redemptive suffering on the cross, so that further confirms that Jesus' sacrifice was sufficient.

We now know what verse 24b doesn't mean in the context of the rest of Scripture which is the most important. There are some varying ideas on what it does mean. Some think it could refer to what is called the messianic woes in Ezekiel 38, Daniel 12:1-3 and Matthew 24:4-14—times of strife for the people of God before Jesus' second coming and the resurrection of the dead. Another thought is connected to Jesus telling Paul that his persecution of the church was actually against Jesus Himself (Acts 9:4). Paul is then sharing in

Christ's afflictions as he takes a stand for the gospel and suffers for it. This portion of verse 24 may well be one we won't fully understand until heaven.

Whatever the meaning of verse 24 we know that it was done for the body of Christ, the church, and as we see in verse 25, Paul was given stewardship of the church by God with the main purpose of making God's Word known. First, Paul uses the word *minister* or *servant*. To Gentiles, a servant was an unskilled, lowly position. God doesn't do things the world's way, though. Jesus was a servant. He taught His disciples to be servants, and Paul was not ashamed to be God's servant.

Paul also uses the word *steward*. This was his, and God's, view of ministry. The church is the household of God (1 Timothy 3:15). Just like a steward of a household, Paul was tasked by God to manage, care for, feed and lead the church, ultimately accountable before God for his stewardship. Paul's greatest burden of stewardship was making the Word of God fully known. He taught the whole counsel of God and had a single-minded focus in fulfilling this responsibility.

Verses 26 and 27 give additional detail on what Paul was making fully known—*the mystery*. The false teachers liked to promise "mysteries" that would be revealed to only a select group. Part of the mystery Paul shared was that it was for everyone, Jewish and Gentile believers. The Old Testament was filled with prophecies and references to the Messiah, but here Paul gives the full revelation: "Christ in you, the hope of glory."

For us now, this may not seem like a very grandiose revelation, but for those in Paul's time, it was huge. Gentiles were unclean. Jews were not to intermarry with Gentiles. Gentiles being included in God's plan was the rare exception not the rule (i.e. In the Old Testament, a Hebrew from Bethlehem, Judah married Ruth, a Moabitess. Ruth was faithful to her mother-in-law and God when both their husbands died. God chose to use Ruth in the lineage of King David and consequently as Jesus' ancestor.). Through faith in Jesus, Jews and Gentiles by the Holy Spirit indwelling them were full partakers together in God's family. In Christ they have a shared inheritance and future, the hope of glory (Revelation 21). This would have been an incredible encouragement to the Gentiles as it should be to us.

For Reflection: Is fear of suffering or ridicule holding you back from sharing the gospel? What is one specific area you can pray about to speak and act according to the truth that God has given you a Spirit of power, love and self-control not fear?

Is there a person, group of people, denomination or ethnicity that you are not viewing as an equal and valued part of the body of Christ with the same indwelling Spirit that makes you both part of God's family? What will you do today to pursue unity? Perhaps start with thanksgiving for the rich diversity in the body of Christ.

DAY 13

COLOSSIANS 1:28-29

Him we proclaim, warning everyone and teaching everyone with all wisdom, that we may present everyone mature in Christ. For this I toil, struggling with all His energy that He powerfully works within me.

I grew up in San Diego with the beach within a half hour. I love the sound of the waves and the peacefulness of watching them roll in. Now that I live in Montana, one of my favorite vacations is a beach vacation especially in the Hawaiian Islands. We try to get at least a second story condo right on the beach, so we can sit on the balcony and just enjoy. First thing in the morning, we go out snorkeling. With someone unfamiliar with the ocean and snorkeling, there are things I would instruct them on: snorkel when the ocean is calmer (waves stir up the sand and decrease visibility), make sure your mask is tight, most of the time you can just swim using your flippers and not using your arms, take an underwater camera as there are so many beautiful

TARA BARNDT

fish (our favorite place to swim has resident sea turtles too!). For the best experience, I would also warn them about certain things like not touching the coral or the sea turtles. I would definitely warn them if jellyfish have been in the area or a tiger shark. I want their snorkel experience to be the best it can be.

Paul depicts something similar in our verses today. His goal is to present everyone mature in Christ. Remember that the false teachers liked to appeal to an elite group. Their mysteries and knowledge weren't for just anybody. Compare that to Paul's objective. He desired for everyone to have the whole gospel to be mature or complete in Christ (Colossians 2:2). Unlike the false teachers, Paul's message exalted Jesus not himself. Likewise, he sought for believers to be dependent on Jesus not himself.

Paul worked toward his goal through two means: warning and teaching. The Greek word for warning is *noutheteō*. It is comprised of two root words—*noús* meaning *mind* and *títhēmi*

meaning *to place*. We usually consider a warning as having negative connotations, but the combined Greek word has a fuller meaning. Strong's Concordance defines it this way, "(admonish through instruction) especially appeals to the mind, supplying doctrinal and spiritual substance (content). This 'exerts positive pressure' on someone's logic (reasoning), i.e. urging them to choose (turn to) God's best."[22] It further carries the idea of counseling or exhorting. Paul proclaimed Jesus and the gospel, he warned against the lies of the false teachers, he admonished believers caught in sin (just read Corinthians), and he exhorted believers to walk in the truth not just have knowledge of the truth.

The second means Paul exercised was teaching. He taught truth, the gospel, what Jesus has done for us, who He is, who we are in Him and how we respond. Others won't know what truth is or how to live apart from the teaching of God's Word. "Following the

56

apostolic model, we exhort others, whether or not we are ordained pastors, to hold fast to the biblical Jesus in all circumstances (Acts 20:29—31; 1 Cor. 4:14; Heb. 6:1—12). Teaching sets forth Christian truth to edify the body of Christ (1 Tim. 4:13; 2 Tim. 3:16; 2 John 9). All believers have a share in the teaching ministry. Some may be ordained to the teaching office, but all believers, in whom Christ's Word dwells richly, teach and admonish one another in all wisdom, at least informally (Col. 3:16)."[23]

I would be remiss if I didn't highlight verse 29 as well. If you know anything about Paul, you know that he was zealous. He was zealous in persecuting the church, and upon saving faith, he was equally if not more zealous in proclaiming Christ. He didn't do things halfway. The word "toil" means to labor until completely exhausted. I don't picture Paul stopping for a coffee break and putting his feet up unless he was preaching as he did it. The second word to describe his effort in presenting believers mature in Christ is "struggling." The Greek word *agōnizomai* described the effort required for someone to compete in a sports event. Can you pick out an English word in the Greek? Agonize. That should give you an idea of what Paul poured into his ministry. However, Paul makes it abundantly clear that it is by God's energy working powerfully in him that he is able to do what God called him to. Paul is not laboring in his own strength.

For Reflection: Every day we all offer counsel to others on a variety of topics. Your co-worker might come to you with a problem at work involving your boss. A teen may complain about how unfair their parents are. A friend might relate how someone hurt them by something he or she said. Your spouse may look to you for help handling the finances. Will your counsel be Biblical (2 Peter 1:3)? Will it encourage and build up according to truth? Purpose to be intentional in how you respond.

What ministry are you currently doing in your own strength instead of God's? Confess to Him your self-reliance and ask for His strength to go forward. Be encouraged that He has given you the very Spirit to indwell you that raised Christ from the dead (Romans 8:11).

DAY 14

COLOSSIANS 2:1-3, 5

*For I want you to know how great a struggle
I have for you and for those at Laodicea and for all who have not seen
me face to face, that their hearts may be encouraged,
being knit together in love, to reach all the riches of full assurance
of understanding and the knowledge of God's mystery,
which is Christ, in whom are hidden all the treasures of wisdom and
knowledge...For though I am absent in body,
yet I am with you in spirit,rejoicing to see your good order
and the firmness of your faith in Christ.*

My two brothers and I are adopted. This may be why adoption,
orphans or children in foster care are important to me. The ministry
of Show Hope has a special place in my heart partly because of the
testimony of the Steven Curtis Chapman family but also because
of the extensive ministry they have to orphans and helping families

adopt. Regularly on social media they will share about a child in one of Show Hope's care facilities in China that is in need of a forever home. Usually with tears, I spend time thanking God that this child has the safety, medical attention and love that Show Hope provides, and then I pray that they would not only have a family of their own but that they would know their Heavenly Father. My heart breaks for these little ones to know the love of a family as I have.

Maybe you have been touched in a similar way by people connected to a ministry or a missionary you know or maybe those affected by a natural disaster or persecution that you have seen in the news. If so, you can understand at least in part how Paul felt even for those he had only heard of. God can move our hearts to love and pray for those He knows and cares for even if we have never met them.

We ended chapter 1 with Paul's goal of presenting everyone mature in Christ through proclaiming, warning and teaching. In chapter 2, he applies this goal through specific instruction. Before he dives into instruction, he assures them of his care and concern for them, the church in Laodicea and for all the believers whom he has not met (verses 1 and 5).

On Day 12, I mentioned my bout with cancer, and the response of the Pathology Department. I had never met or spoken with anyone in the Pathology Department, yet they heard of my situation and my faith and prayed for me. That was a remarkable encouragement to me. Imagine what it meant to the Colossian believers to know that Paul cared enough for them to not only write but to convey that he was struggling for them, praying for them, was with them in spirit and was rejoicing that they were firm in their faith (which he hoped to see in person).

Paul repeats the word "struggle" (verse 1) that he used in verse 1:29—the agonizing effort to compete in a sports event. The Colossian believers were not just a passing thought to Paul. He was willing to and did suffer and ultimately gave his life for the sake of sharing the gospel and building up believers like the Colossians.

In verse 2 we observe three linked outcomes that Paul struggled to see grow in the Colossian believers. First, that they would be encouraged. Encourage means to comfort or exhort, but the Greek *parakaleō* further has the idea of empowering another to face hardship positively. Can you think of a time when you were discouraged? Often discouragement sets us up as a target. We are more susceptible to believing lies, letting sin into our lives or giving up. Paul taught the Thessalonian church to "encourage one another and build one another up" (1 Thessalonians 5:11). We all can be discouraged at one time or another. God has given us brothers and sisters in Christ to walk with us and build us up with truth when we are discouraged.

Second, we are able to encourage each other when we are knit together in love. Paul is talking about a unity that is rooted in God's love for us and in His truth. I have an antique rocking chair that I inherited from my grandma. The main part of the seat is made from some type of thick grass or straw woven together. I would not typically think that pieces of straw would hold my weight, but woven together, they have a strength they would not otherwise have. Likewise, when we are fueled by God's love for us and grounded in His Word, we can pursue unity with other believers. Everyone will be built up and encouraged.

Third, the culmination of this is that the body reaches "all the riches of full assurance of understanding and the knowledge of God's mystery, which is Christ, in whom are hidden all the treasures of wisdom and knowledge." In the Old Testament we have five books that are referred to as wisdom literature: Job, Psalms, Proverbs, Ecclesiastes and Song of Solomon. They impart direct, wise instruction, reveal things about God's character and His ways, the limits of human wisdom, the marks of a wise person and depictions of the coming Messiah. These books of the Bible and the wisdom they contain are still valuable to us today (1 Corinthians 10:11).

In verses 2 and 3, we see an astounding revelation about wisdom. The Old Testament revealed types and shadows of the coming Messiah. In the New Testament the Messiah came. We today have the fullness of Jesus incarnate (in human form) as revealed in the Scriptures (John 1:17), and Paul tells us that in Jesus all the treasures of wisdom and knowledge are hidden.

"He is our wisdom unto salvation, the final goal of the Wisdom Literature. If we read and apply the Wisdom Books in light of the person and work of Jesus Christ, foolishness and death will never lay a permanent hold on us."[24]

In Christ, we have the assurance of salvation. We have understanding of Jesus incarnate (1 Timothy 3:16) and the gospel. We have access to the One who has all wisdom and knowledge, and Who has given us His Spirit so we might understand.

Again, we see Paul's deliberate choice of words in the use of hidden. The Gnostics, one group of false teachers, believed that someone needed to amass great stores of knowledge to be saved. They gathered this knowledge in a set of books, but the average person was not allowed access to this knowledge. The Gnostics hid it. Paul's use of hidden is a jab at them. Think of a treasure chest filled with gold and jewels. You can open the chest and have access to the treasure. The treasure chest is simply where the treasure is stored. Wisdom and knowledge are stored as a treasure in Jesus, and anyone can have access to Jesus by faith. Wisdom and knowledge are not just teachings. They are the person of Jesus. Paul affirms that everything is loss compared to the surpassing worth of knowing Jesus (Philippians 3:7-11).

There are two words in today's verses that I especially love—riches (verse 2) and treasures (verse 3). These words bring to mind two movie series—*Pirates of the Caribbean* and *Raiders of the Lost Ark*. The characters in both are seeking some sort of treasure. They are willing to risk everything (except maybe Indy's love interest) to find the treasure. It is precious and valuable. Worth sacrificing for. How much more so the treasure of Jesus Himself and the wisdom and knowledge hidden in Him? We begin to experience the riches and treasures of Christ as we are "knit together in love" and unified with other believers.

For Reflection: Think of a people group somewhere around the world (or your own neighborhood) that you don't know. It could be someone a missionary that you support knows, Christians being persecuted for their faith, someone affected by a natural disaster or a ministry you know of. Spend time in prayer for them today. You can pray for spiritual, emotional and physical needs. Pray for their hearts to be encouraged. You might want to incorporate this into your regular prayer time.

Do you see Jesus and the wisdom and knowledge hidden in Him as a treasure? Are you willing to sacrifice to seek Him and the wisdom found in Him? I know the right answer is yes, but my life doesn't always reflect that. If you are like me, ask God to give you a love for Jesus and His truth. Ask for an anticipation each day to read His Word. Psalm 119 is a great place to spur you on to a love of God's Word.

DAY 15

COLOSSIANS 2:6-7

Therefore, as you received Christ Jesus the Lord,
so walk in Him, rooted and built up in Him and established in the faith,
just as you were taught, abounding in thanksgiving.

Recently a family we knew during our time in Oklahoma lost their sixteen-year-old son in a football accident. I was able to watch the memorial service on the church's website. The Dad and the four other sons (teenagers or college-age) all shared. As I listened, I heard their memories and their grief, but overriding all of it was their unwavering faith in a faithful, loving, good and sovereign God. Even in that first week after their son and brother's death, the family was already seeking how to respond to their loss in a way that glorified God. This doesn't mean they weren't grieving and feeling the loss of their son and brother, but it is evidence that this family is rooted, built up in Christ and established in their faith (God's Word). It isn't faith hinging on a quick in and out at church on Sunday morning while sneaking peeks at text messages. It is a faith they have walked in over many years at church, home, work and school.

Paul charges the Colossian believers not to be deluded (verse 4) or deceived (verse 8) by things that might sound good but are actually of no value and based on man's thinking. Yesterday we studied Paul's desire for the Colossians to be encouraged (verse 2). We know that we are more susceptible to lies, plausible arguments and man's empty deceit and traditions when we are discouraged. As I think of my friends, I know they will face well-meaning people who will not encourage them with truth. "Why would God let your son die at an early age? He can't be good. Aren't you mad at God for what He allowed to happen?" People have human solutions they turn to like drinking, hardening their hearts towards loving others, throwing themselves into a hobby or work or leaving the church. I am thankful for Paul's words and the example of our friends. It is only by God's grace and being rooted and built up in Jesus and established in the faith that we can not only stand firm when the trials, discouragement, lies and deception come, but we can also abound in thanksgiving through it.

As we have already studied, the false teachers offered new, secret knowledge. Paul tells the Colossian believers that they have already received what they need to know. They do not need something new or different. They have their roots, their grounding. Adding to the gospel message is to deny the sufficiency of Christ. John MacArthur addresses a similar attack today in the church with false philosophy in the guise of psychology being seen as a necessary addition to God's Word. Others look to visions, rely on the law for holiness, practice asceticism or add man-made requirements to salvation. They all equate to the same—denying the sufficiency of Christ.

It is Christ's finished, complete, sufficient work on the cross that is the one and only thing we need to be rooted, built up and established in the faith. Everything else flows from the foundation of the gospel or it is false. I can imagine that part of what sustained my friends in their grief was the truth that God out of love for us gave His only Son to die in order to redeem us and make His own. Because of Jesus' death and resurrection, their son and brother received forgiveness, was saved and is eternally with the Father. They have the sure and steadfast hope that they will see him again.

The Greek word for "received" described receiving something by way of a tradition. Paul told the Colossian church that they had received Jesus Himself as the tradition. They didn't just receive a teaching or an abstract idea. They received Jesus Himself. As Paul then urges the Colossians to continue to walk (daily conduct) in the faith that they had started with (received), they do this knowing that Jesus is with them. He's with you. Don't look for something new or additional. What you have is all you need. Your life is to be patterned after Jesus' life.

"Our Savior calls us to obedience, not that we might earn our salvation but that we may display our gratitude for His grace. If we love Him—if we have love for God poured into our hearts (Rom. 5:5)—we will keep His commandments, which are not burdensome (John 14:15; 1 John 5:3)."[25]

As you might guess, "rooted" is an agricultural concept. We know that roots nourish and anchor the plant. A plant would not last long without roots. It would be plucked up, blown away or simply die. In a similar way, we need to have our roots deeply planted in Jesus and the Word in order to stand firm and grow. If we do not have deep roots in God's character and His Word, when trials hit, we will be deceived (verse 8) and turn from truth.

"Built up" is an architectural term. Jesus, the message of the gospel and the teaching of the apostles is our foundation ("established in the faith"). Out of that foundation we mature spiritually. The word *taught* reminds us that it is by God's Word that we are strengthened, nourished and built up. Epaphras had faithfully taught the Colossian church. Today we have the whole of Scripture to study on our own and to learn from during corporate worship.

The final aspect of Paul's description of walking in Christ in this section is that we abound in thanksgiving. The Greek word for *abounding* portrays a rushing river that overflows its banks. Before I started my thankful journal, my thanksgiving typically was limited to major events (like a near-miss car accident). The more purposeful I am in being thankful, the more material and spiritual blessings come to mind. It is a process, but one worth pursuing.

My friends in Oklahoma are just one example of walking in Christ, being rooted and built up in Him, being established in the faith and abounding in thanksgiving. Singer Steven Curtis Chapman and his family are another faithful example (read their story if you don't know it). Hebrews 11 is filled with rooted, established, faithful people. You may know your own examples. I pray you will be rooted and built up in Christ, established in the faith, abounding in thanksgiving.

For Reflection: Building on yesterday's reflection, I would encourage you to find an accountability partner for studying God's Word as this is a struggle for many believers to be consistent. Lately, I have been changing how I check in with our youth group kids. Instead of simply asking them if they have done devotions (this can produce more guilt than encouragement or a check-list mentality), I have been asking them what they have been learning. What is something cool that has stood out to them? Yes or no answers won't help build each other up. Sharing what we are learning does. It is a way of meditating on Scripture as well.

There are many ways to approach our quiet time. Prayer is a great way to start although there is not a set formula for quiet time. Prayer is important on its own for connecting with God, but we can also pray that God would open our minds and hearts to what He wants to teach us as we read Scripture. Prayer can remind us that the purpose of a quiet time is to know God more intimately not acquire Biblical facts.

Some like using a devotional book like this (make sure the devotional gets you into the Word). Others prefer reading Scripture alone. Some highlight as they read, make verse cards or journal. With journaling there are many options too (i.e., writing out the attributes or characteristics of God, things to praise God for, things to obey, where you see Jesus in the passage, etc.). Others may write out what they learn in a poem or a song or even act or dance it out. For some it is easier to listen to the Bible, a book or a sermon. Explore what works best for you. Start with something manageable. Set yourself up for success not discouragement. Katie Orr has some wonderful suggestions on her website https://resources.katieorr.me/passes.

Keep in mind that your quiet time will likely change over the years. Different seasons of life might bring more or less time. I've met many young mothers that were discouraged because they didn't have a long period of time to spend with God anymore. That's ok. God is not counting the minutes. He just wants to spend time with you. There are times I concentrate on one book of the Bible. Other times I read sections from ten different books of the Bible each day which has helped me better see of the whole of Scripture. Sometimes I've included books or Scripture-rich devotionals.

Is your thanksgiving more of a trickle or a rushing river or somewhere in between? Keep adding to your thankful journal and continue cultivating an overflowing heart of thanksgiving.

DAY 16

COLOSSIANS 2:4, 8

I say this in order that no one may delude you with plausible arguments…See to it that no one takes you captive by philosophy and empty deceit, according to human tradition, according to the elemental spirits of the world, and that according to Christ.

My husband has been known to say that the best lies contain a certain amount of truth. Truth mixed with a lie makes it more believable. Throw in a little truth or even a lot and the deception won't set off alarms.

I was trying to think of an example in my own life as I know I've allowed myself to be duped more than once in my life, but two Biblical examples came to mind right away. The first was in the beginning… The serpent, or Satan, comes to Eve in the garden. He is described as being craftier than any other beast. He said to Eve, "Did God actually say, 'You shall not eat of *any* tree in the garden'?"

(Genesis 3:1). Phrasing it this way makes it seem nigh impossible that God would actually command such a thing. It is as if God would be cruel to forbid eating the fruit, and Eve would know that God was not cruel. The serpent also framed his words to be similar to what God had said with a few important tweaks.

God had said, "You may surely eat of *every* tree of the garden, but of the tree of the knowledge of good and evil you shall not eat, for in the day that you eat of it you shall surely die" (Genesis 2:16-17). God was incredibly generous in what He gave Adam and Eve to partake from. Out of all created trees, there was only one that God said they weren't to eat from. Two words—*any* and *every*—but a monumental difference in truth. Eve sinned and was deceived because she failed to stand firm in what she knew about God.

The second example is probably familiar as well and is found in the gospels of Matthew, Mark and Luke. The scene is set when the Spirit leads Jesus to the wilderness to fast for forty days and nights and then be tempted by the devil (Matthew 4:1-2). As you can imagine, Jesus was famished by the end. Do you remember on Day 14 from Colossians 2:2 where Paul desired the Colossian believers to be encouraged because when we are discouraged, we are more susceptible to temptation? I know my susceptibility rises with skipping one meal. I can't imagine how discouraged and susceptible I would be after forty days of fasting.

In Satan's first two attempts, he began with, "If (or since) you are the Son of God..." Satan knew that Jesus was the Son of God. He tried to take the truth of Jesus' identity as the Son of God and use it to manipulate or deceive Jesus into doing what he wanted. In each of the three temptations, unlike Eve, Jesus responds with truth and obedience to the Father's will. He quotes Scripture. On the second temptation, Satan attempted to be even more devious by also quoting Scripture, adding that bit of truth to his deceptive temptation. Jesus saw right through that ploy and again responded with Scripture but in the correct context. In Jesus' response to the third temptation, He not only counters with Scripture, but He tells Satan to be gone!

Can you see why Paul began chapter 2 (our divisions not Paul's) the way he did? It is essential that we are encouraged, knit together in love with other believers, having the wisdom, knowledge and understanding that are in Christ, walking in Christ, being rooted, built up and established in our faith and abounding in thanksgiving. Then we will not be taken captive by deception no matter how good it sounds. We will recognize and combat the lies because we know truth. Later we will read in Colossians 4:5-6 that Paul commands us to conduct ourselves wisely towards outsiders, make the best use of the time, and let our speech be gracious and seasoned with salt so that we will know how to answer everyone.

Jesus did this perfectly in every instance. He knew the Scriptures, so He was prepared to combat temptations and deceit. We too need to be prepared with a ready answer.

Let's break down our two verses a little more. Paul is warning the Colossian believers to be vigilant. He didn't believe they had already succumbed to deceit, but he knew the danger of being unprepared. He tells the Colossian church that the arguments would sound plausible. My husband went to a Christian university. For chapel one week, they brought in two speakers: one argued creation, the other argued creative evolution (a view that seeks to combine the ideas of creation with that of evolution). In this case, the one arguing creative evolution did a better job than the creationist. Hence, his argument sounded totally plausible. Even so, my husband was not swayed from what he had studied in Scripture.

Universities and colleges are fertile grounds for many plausible arguments. Studies show between sixty and eighty-eight percent of children from evangelical homes turn from their faith during their young adult years. Without the grounding in Scripture and the tight knitting together with other believers, the worldview taught in our schools and supported by peers will seem plausible. Attending church or youth group weekly or having Christian friends is not necessarily the rooted foundation young adults need. For further information, Answers in Genesis published an insightful article on this.[26]

The term "take captive" was used for theft. Paul is illustrating what the false teachers wanted to do—rob the Colossian believers of the truth they knew. He lists four methods they used. The first is through philosophy which simply means a "love of wisdom". That isn't bad if it is God's wisdom we are loving, but during Paul's era, philosophy had a more expansive meaning. It could include almost any theory. Paul's use of it in verse 8 is referring to the false teaching particularly about the sufficiency of Christ. The false teaching might have been a combination of Gnosticism and Jewish mysticism, but regardless of the specifics, this philosophy did not magnify Jesus which secondly made it empty deceit. It had no value.

False teaching was according to human tradition. It was from man not God. Your church may have certain traditions like a benediction at the end of the service or having a Christmas Eve service, but we must be careful that man-made traditions are not being made equal or superior to Scripture or that they are not contrary to Scripture. God's Word is the ultimate authority.

Fourth, Paul refers to "elemental spirits of the world." The Greek *stoicheia* had multiple applications, and theologians classify its use in verse 8 under "interpretive difficulties." One thought is that Paul had in mind regional gods (similar concept in 2 Kings 17:26-29). Other prevalent spirits were the gods of the stars, planets and even of the physical elements. Jewish teaching combined angels and astral powers who protected the planets. We would know them as demons that sought to enslave under the guise of freeing a person (1 Corinthians 10:1-22). When we reach verse 2:18, Paul again mentions elemental spirits.

The King James translates this phrase as "the rudiments of the world." The second school of thought is that *stoicheia* refers to basic elements of learning, rudimentary teachings. This definition could tie to 2:16-19 where we see false teachers promoted dietary restrictions and observing specific calendar dates as a means of salvation or sanctification. Either way, it boils down to Jesus plus _____ (fill in the blank) mentality. Believers need Jesus plus intermediary beings or specific practices. Scripture teaches Christ alone.

Paul ends his sentence contrasting the four deceptive methods of taking us captive with "and not according to Christ." This is the crux of the matter. If it doesn't align with Christ, what is in Scripture or what the gospel message proclaims, it is false.

For Reflection: In the Old Testament God commanded certain dietary laws and rituals (specific sacrifices, cleansing laws, etc.), so we know that those kinds of things or traditions are not bad in themselves. They become sin when they are the end answer to our holiness in place of Jesus and the Spirit's work. We fall into this thinking when we make rules about and base our holiness on particular ways to worship or specific things we can or cannot watch, listen to or participate in. What in your life have you made into Jesus plus _____? If you are to put the "Jesus plus _____" off, what truths would help you replace that thinking? (For example: Jesus plus so-and-so's approval. Truth: Luke 12:47—fear God not man who can only affect our physical body. Genesis 1:26-27—you are made in God's image therefore, you have value. Romans 8:31-32, 35-37—God is for you. He loves you unconditionally and nothing can separate you from His love.

DAY 17

COLOSSIANS 2:9-10

For in Him the whole fullness of deity dwells bodily, and you have been filled in Him who is the head of all rule and authority.

Growing up, my family moved six times. I am more of an introvert so making friends at a new school was not easy for me. Near the end of middle school, we moved into a different high school district than my friends. Five or six weeks into my freshman year, I came down with mono. I was out of school the rest of the semester, finishing my classes via a tutor who came to the house to drop off and pick up my homework.

I was thankful to have mono and not have to go back to a school where I didn't really know anyone. I could usually get all my work done in an hour or two and spent the rest of the time (confession one) watching soap operas and other tv. By second semester, I was well enough to return to school, but I didn't want to. My parents gave me the option of going to a Christian school or staying where I was. I figured anything had to be better than where I was. Of course, that meant being new again.

The freshman class at the public high school was around five hundred. The freshman class at the Christian school was twenty-eight. No getting lost there. Two girls befriended me the very first day. One of them is still a very dear friend over thirty-five years later. I really wanted to impress these two new friends with how popular I was with guys, so I made up a story and forged letters (confession two) from a guy I had actually had a crush on during the two years we lived in Boise. (I am a native San Diegan, but we lived for two years in Idaho during my fifth and sixth grade years.) I embellished a lot including that this guy was "giving" me one of their racehorses although the horse would stay in Idaho. It was the stuff teen girl dreams are made of. However, on one letter I forgot to alter my handwriting when I signed the guy's name. One of my friends recognized my writing, and the charade was over. I was not who I claimed to be. Thankfully my friends did not unfriend me.

At one time or another, we all have someone we put on a pedestal that ends up disappointing us or we pretend to be someone we are not. In verse 9 today we see what might seem to be an unbelievable claim, "For in Him the whole fullness of deity dwells bodily". Jesus possessed absolutely everything that God is, every attribute, every iota of God's being in His human body—fully God, fully human. This is not an embellishment, lie or figment of Paul's imagination. Jesus is who the Scriptures say He is.

If you grew up in the church, this is probably not a new concept although it can be difficult to wrap our limited minds around. How can fully God be perfectly united with fully human? Back on Day 7, we talked about creeds. The Heidelberg Catechism explains Jesus' deity and humanity.

"Q & A 48: Q. If His humanity is not present wherever His divinity is, then aren't the two natures of Christ separated from each other? A. Certainly not. Since divinity is not limited and is present everywhere (Jeremiah 23:23-24; Acts 7:48-49; Isaiah 66:1), it is evident that Christ's divinity is surely beyond the bounds of the humanity that has been taken on, but at the same time His divinity is in and remains personally united to His humanity (John 1:14; 3:13; Colossians 2:9)."[27]

The Nicene Creed further affirms Jesus' deity, "God of God, Light of Light, very God of very God, begotten, not made, being of one substance of the Father, by whom all things were made."[28]

We have touched on this already, but to refresh our memories, we learned that the false teachers believed the human body was evil, the spirit was good, and Jesus was really just a lesser spirit deriving from God. Paul, as in 1:15-19, asserts the truth of Jesus' full deity and humanity together in his earthly body. Having a human body does not negate Jesus' deity.

By the phrase, "filled in Him," we know Christ is sufficient for all we need. "Believers are made complete in Christ by the imputed perfect righteousness of Christ and through the complete sufficiency of all heavenly resources needed for spiritual maturity."[29] The world's empty philosophy and deceit deny the sufficiency of Jesus. Paul, as well as Peter, contradicts that thinking with the truth that in Jesus alone we possess everything we need for life and godliness (2 Peter 1:3).

We are filled not by our own endeavors but by the indwelling of the Holy Spirit, who by the same power that raised Jesus from the dead, enables us to live a life of godliness and gives us understanding of God's Word. Knowing this allows us to enjoy what God has given us by His grace, and to walk in Christ (verse 6) out of gratitude to and love for God.

Paul further describes Jesus, with whom we are filled, as the "head of all rule and authority." He counters the false teaching of Jesus being a lesser spirit deriving from God. Paul declares that Jesus is the Head, He is Creator and Ruler, He is before all things, all things are held together by Him, He is preeminent (1:18). "Rule and authority" echoes Paul's statement in 1:16. Pagans believed spiritual beings ruled their lives. Paul asserts that Jesus being preeminent rules over everything and everyone. Paul wrote to the Philippian church, "that at the name of Jesus every knee should bow, in heaven and on earth and under the earth, and every tongue confess that Jesus Christ is Lord, to the glory of God the Father" (Philippians 2:10-11).

For Reflection: Have you ever paused to really meditate on what it means for Jesus to be fully man and yet fully God? In His human body, Jesus faced all the limits and frailties of a man, and although He was also fully God, He did not use His divinity to squash limitations in His humanity. Take some time to list aspects of Jesus' humanity, what He experienced the same as you and I and thank Him for His willingness to humble Himself to be fully human. Then write out some of the attributes of God, which Jesus completely possessed, and how you see those in Jesus' life as well.

If you want to study this more, *God Is: A Devotional Guide to the Attributes of God* by Mark Jones[30] is a great resource. Each chapter details the doctrine behind each of God's attributes, how that attribute is exhibited in Jesus and how it applies to us.

DAY 18

COLOSSIANS 2:11-15

*In Him also you were circumcised with a circumcision
made without hands, by putting off the body of the flesh,
by the circumcision of Christ, having been buried with Him in baptism,
in which you were also raised with Him through faith in the powerful
working of God, who raised Him from the dead. And you,
who were dead in your trespasses and the uncircumcision
of your flesh, God made alive together with Him, having forgiven
us all our trespasses, by canceling the record of debt that stood
against us with its legal demands. This He set aside,
nailing it to the cross. He disarmed the rulers and authorities and put
them to open shame, by triumphing over them in Him.*

My grandpa instilled in me a love of sports and in particular a
love for my San Diego/Southern California teams—the Lakers, Padres
and Chargers (before they defected to Los Angeles). When I spent

time at my grandparents' house, it seems like Grandpa always had a game playing on the radio. It is one of my fondest memories of him.

Although the Padres made it to the World Series twice, they lost both times. Not much to celebrate. My husband and one of my closest friends are Cubs' fans. There seems to be a uniqueness to Cubs' fans as a whole, a connection to the Cubs that is more than an average sports fan. In the 2016 season, the Cubs had gone one hundred eight years without winning the World Series. It is the longest drought not only in Major League Baseball but also in all North American Sports. You can imagine the excitement and anticipation when the Cubs made it to the World Series that year.

For those who aren't familiar with baseball or the World Series, the team that wins four games out of seven is the champion. In 2016, the Chicago Cubs and Cleveland Indians met on the ballfield. The series was not looking good for the Cubs when Cleveland took a 3-1 game lead. The Cubs rallied the next two games to tie up at three games to three games. One game left to decide it all.

The tension going into Game 7 was escalated. The Cubs launched into an early lead in the first inning, but any true Cubs' fan knows that it is too early to get excited, and they were proved right in the eighth inning. They had a 6-3 lead going into the bottom of the eighth but gave up three runs including a homerun. Cubs' hearts sank as they thought, "Here we go again." The Cubs then wasted a scoring opportunity in the top of the ninth inning which could've won the game for them. Instead it pushed the game into an extra inning with a tie of 6-6 at the bottom of the ninth (game is typically over in nine innings unless tied).

As if this wasn't enough to keep fans from both sides on the edge of their seats, there was a seventeen-minute rain delay right before the tenth inning. At the top of the tenth, the Cubs were up to bat first. They scored two runs and now had an 8-6 lead, but

Cleveland still had their turn at bat. They scored a run but had two outs. I'm sure everyone was holding their breath as the next Cleveland batter came up to home plate. The pitch. A grounder hit. Cubs' player Bryant fielded and threw it to Rizzo at first base. OUT! The Cubs win the World Series 8-7! Can you imagine the celebration after waiting one hundred eight years for that win? Some Cubs' fans still tear up when they remember the final victory. It was a monumental day of triumph for Cubs' fans and led to an estimated five million fans (nearly two times Chicago's population) in attendance at the Cubs' victory parade.

That may have been a long introduction especially if you aren't a baseball fan, but it was the most recent massive celebration I could think of. I wanted to try to build the emotion, or I'd be in trouble with all the Cubs' fans out there. As thrilling as that win was for Cubs' fans, today's verses spotlight the most amazing triumph in all of history that is worthy of continual celebration. Death to life. Forgiveness. Rulers and authorities disarmed and put to shame. Jesus' triumph through His death, burial and resurrection. That is the best news that should never cease to be celebrated or given thanks for.

We'll begin with verse 11 and work our way through the many reasons we have to celebrate. In the Old Testament originating with Abraham, God instituted the symbol of circumcision. There was the outward sign of the physical cutting of the flesh setting them apart as God's people as well as serving as a reminder that the Israelites would be cut off if they broke the covenant. Paul tells the Colossian believers that in Christ, they have been circumcised but not by hands. Paul is referring to the circumcision of the heart. Although God commanded the physical circumcision of the Israelites, what was most important was the circumcision of the heart (Deuteronomy 10:12-22).

Paul describes the circumcision of the heart first by the "putting off of the body of flesh". The Greek word for *putting off* is a double compound. Like the imagery of dirty clothes, it describes both peeling off and throwing aside. This is what is done with our flesh or sinful nature. Second, this "putting off the body of flesh" occurs only in those who are in Christ. Jesus' death, burial and resurrection accomplished what the law could not. Jesus' broke the power of sin in our lives. Although we continue to sin, sin has no power over us. God has provided a way of escape from and a way to stand up under the temptation to sin (1 Corinthians 10:13).

In verse 12, Paul switches to the picture of baptism. I understand this can be a touchy subject for some as there are different views surrounding baptism. We will focus on Paul's purpose in this context. It may be of interest to note that in addition to the correlation to water, the Greek for baptism can also be used figuratively for identification with something or someone. The latter is how Paul applies it in verse 12. In fact, the Greek verbs for buried, raised and alive (verses 12-13) would be better translated as co-buried, co-raised and co-alive. Paul states that we are identified with Jesus in His burial, resurrection and resurrected life.

Our identification with Jesus' burial reflects sin being conquered. Because of Jesus' atonement, sin no longer holds power over our lives. The old nature, reflected in the description "dead in our trespasses" (sin) and "uncircumcision of our flesh", is put to death and buried. Being dead in our trespasses depicts the extent to our enslavement to sin and our hopelessness (Ephesians 2:12). We had no spiritual life (1 Corinthians 2:14) and were unable to respond to God at all until His Spirit worked in us as seen by "God made alive".

The Heidelberg Catechism puts it this way, "That by His power our old man is with Him crucified, slain and buried; that so the evil lusts of the flesh may no more reign in us, but that we may offer ourselves unto Him a sacrifice of thanksgiving" (A. 43).[31]

Not only is our sin nature put to death and buried, but in Christ we are raised to a new life, we are a new creation (2 Corinthians 5:17). Further, we were made alive *together with Him.* In the introduction, I encouraged you to use the chart in Appendix A to list all the phrases of "in Him" or "with Him" and the corresponding blessing. Here is one of those phrases. I like how Charles Spurgeon highlights the importance of "with Him" in this verse.

"It is true that He gave us life from the dead. He gave us pardon of sin; He gave us imputed righteousness. These are all precious things, but you see we are not content with them; we have received Christ Himself. The Son of God has been poured out into us, and we have received Him, and appropriated Him."[32] Do you see that the ultimate blessing is being alive *with Christ*? Being alive without Christ is not really being alive.

Our quote from Spurgeon touched on other blessings of being alive with Christ. The Greek for *forgiven* (verse 13a) is *charizomai.* On Day 1 we studied different forms of the Greek word *charis.* This is another one, and it gets at the heart of Scripture—God's free grace of forgiveness and redemption for those who put their trust in Jesus' atoning work on the cross (Romans 3:24; 5:20; Ephesians 1:7). Forgiveness is ours with Him.

In addition to being forgiven, God has canceled our debt, a debt we would never be able to repay (Galatians 3:10; James 2:10; Matthew 18:23-29). "Record of debt" was a business term. A certificate of the debt was written by the debtor's own hand often on parchment that could be washed off when the debt was paid. It could also refer to the confession of or the charges brought against a prisoner. Either use is a reminder that everyone is a debtor to God under the Law.

With Christ, the grace abounds. Jesus canceled our debt, but in addition He set its condemnation aside where it will never hold dominion over us again (Romans 6:14; 7:6). Jesus fulfilled the law perfectly making a way for us to walk in His righteousness by the Spirit's power. Then, He nailed our debt to the cross. In Paul's day, a criminal's crimes were written out and nailed to the cross with him so everyone would know what he had done. For believers, all our sins were nailed to Jesus' cross, they were put to His account. He paid the penalty. God's just wrath has been satisfied.

Verse 15 concludes this section with a resounding victory. Jesus' death on the cross signaled Satan's defeat (Hebrews 2:14). Satan had the power of death after tempting Adam and Eve to sin. His power over death could be defeated only by a just penalty being paid. Jesus accomplished that for us. Satan can no longer threaten believers with death and eternal separation from God. He can no longer bring condemnation (Romans 8:33-39). Although Satan's power is broken (disarmed), spiritual battles are still waged until Jesus' return (Ephesians 6:10-18; 1 Peter 5:8).

Paul's words depict that of conquering Roman generals. The custom was to parade the defeated through the streets. Leading up to Jesus' death, this is a picture of what is happening. Jesus was humiliated, beaten, spit on, paraded through Jerusalem, stripped naked and then crucified publicly. Like a general, Satan must have thought he'd achieved IT! He had defeated the Son of God, but God flipped things around. What Satan thought was his victory was God's plan from eternity to triumph over Satan, sin and death by Jesus' own righteous, atoning death and resurrection. Yes, we will have the celebration of all celebrations when Jesus returns and has the final victory, but right now, today, is a day to celebrate too.

For Reflection: What facets of being made alive with Christ are you most thankful for?

Take some time to reflect on the enormous blessing of being *with Him*—we have access to intimate, personal fellowship with Jesus now.

Are there specific areas you are succumbing to Satan's condemnation? Meditate on our verses today with thanksgiving that Satan has no power over you. God is for you. Who can be against you? The Father gave His own Son so that He could graciously give you all things. Who can bring any charge against you who are God's elect? It is God who justifies.

If you can, listen to "Best News Ever" by MercyMe. It's a great reminder of what we've talked about today and a good preparation for tomorrow.

DAY 19

COLOSSIANS 2:16-19

*Therefore let no one pass judgment on you in questions
of food and drink, or with regard to a festival or a new moon
or a Sabbath. These are a shadow of the things to come,
but the substance belongs to Christ. Let no one disqualify you,
insisting on asceticism and worship of angels, going on in detail about
visions, puffed up without reason by his sensuous mind,
and not holding fast to the Head, from whom the whole body,
nourished and knit together through its joints and ligaments,
grows with a growth that is from God.*

Have you ever belonged to a club or maybe joined a gym? My experience takes me back to when I was nine years old. We lived in a newly built neighborhood. My best friend Tammy lived down the street on Terra Circle. I don't think either of us was allowed to watch *Charlies' Angels* (the original, the only, and yes, that dates me), but

I would sneak up while Mom was at ladies' Bible study and watch it almost to the end when she would come home. The Angels were brave and beautiful. I wanted to be an Angel, so Tammy and I formed our own little Angel club. As we didn't have a Pinto or a Cobra to drive, we had to settle for bikes. We had to be girls. We had to have an Angel persona (I was Kelly because she had brown hair like mine). We had to keep our investigations secret, and for exclusivity, your name had to begin with a T or that's just how it worked out. There were undeveloped lots near us, and when we could get out of the house, we'd ride our bikes down there, collect clues and keep our eyes peeled on suspicious looking cars and people going by. To this day, Tammy and I are the only ones who know the sinister things that transpired.

Your club might not have been as exciting as mine and Tammy's was, but there is still something they have in common: rules and requirements. There weren't other kids in the neighborhood our age, so we never had to disqualify someone. In Paul's day, the false teachers were trying to do precisely that. Paul sets the record straight.

Before we go too far, did you notice the *therefore* in our verses today? *Therefore* points us back to what we studied yesterday or the message in "Best News Ever" if you were able to listen to it. The fight has already been won. The work has already been done. Jesus accomplished everything we needed. He was triumphant. *Therefore* let no one pass judgment on you, disqualify you or enslave you ("submit to regulations" in verses 20-23). We have our foundation. We have our hope. We know the truth. In Jesus, we can say no to those who say we need to do more even if that is our own voice.

Paul attacks the heresy of legalism because at its core, legalism is denying the sufficiency of Jesus' atonement (verses 11-15). Those trying to pass judgment on the Colossian believers insisted that following their rules and traditions to regulate outward behaviors determined one's salvation and righteousness. This reminds me of Jesus confronting the Pharisees. "Woe to you, scribes and Pharisees, hypocrites! For you are like whitewashed tombs, which outwardly appear beautiful, but within are full of dead people's bones and all uncleanness. So you also outwardly appear righteous to others, but within you are full of hypocrisy and lawlessness" (Matthew 23:27-28).

Earlier in verses 4 and 8 Paul warned the Colossian believers not to be taken captive by plausible arguments, philosophy and empty deceit that is based on human tradition. This form of legalism is exactly that. It looks oh so good on the outside. See my self-restraint and strict adherence to the rules? It sounds good, plausible, and holy. We think, "I can do this. I can control this. I can look righteous to others and God." But the deceitfulness of this is that it is only external, we can never be righteous enough before a holy God, and it shifts our trust from God to self. Timothy Keller commenting on Romans 4:1-5 calls this a "trust transfer". Saving faith is transferring our trust in our own works to trusting in Jesus' finished work on the cross. Now these false teachers are maneuvering to get the Colossian believers to reverse that trust transfer back to works (Galatians 2:16). In Romans Paul outlines the marks of a true Christian not as one who religiously follows outward rules, but as one whose love is genuine (12:9-21) and who displays the fruit of the Spirit (Galatians 5:22-25).

Paul targets some of the specific, man-made regulations. He covers food, drink, festivals, a new moon and a Sabbath. The Mosaic law had requirements for all these, but they were shadows of what was to come—Jesus. Now that we have the true substance, we don't need the shadows. Paul told Timothy, "For everything created by God is good, and nothing is rejected if it is received with thanksgiving, for it is made holy by the word of God and prayer" (1 Timothy 4:4-5). Peter was told in Acts 10:15, "What God has made clean, do not call common." Jesus Himself in response to the Pharisees condemning His disciples for picking and eating grain on the Sabbath said, "For the Son of Man is lord of the Sabbath" (Matthew 12:8). Again, Paul asserts that Jesus is enough. Why choose a shadow when we have all we need in Jesus?

Paul continues with the warning to let no one disqualify you. The Greek *katabrabeuō* would be similar to a referee or an umpire making a call against a player like a penalty or a foul. More specifically the player was deprived of his prize. Paul does not mean that a believer can lose his/her salvation, but God does reward us in heaven (1 Corinthians 3:8, 14). We can lose rewards from our lack of labor or laboring after the wrong things. Paul underscores other forms of legalism that disregard the sufficiency of Jesus.

False teachers were insisting on asceticism which can mean a strict self-discipline like the regulations on food, drink, festivals, new moon or the Sabbath, but the Greek can also refer to humility and is translated that way in some Bible versions. Yes, believers are to be humble just as Jesus was (Philippians 2:5-8), but the kind of humility the false teachers insisted on was not modeled after Jesus. It was not for looking to other's interest. It actually called attention to their own false humility and righteousness.

The worship of angels was a pagan practice that afflicted the area around Colossae for centuries. Gnostics believed that God was so far elevated above man that He could be worshipped solely through angels. Not only is this practice prohibited in Scripture (Matthew 4:10; Revelation 19:10; 22:8-9), but it denies Jesus as the one, true and only Mediator between God and man (1 Timothy 2:5).

Paul's last attack is against visions. Again, this was something the Gnostics practiced. It was a source of pride to receive this special information that others didn't. These mystical experiences with the spirit world were separate from God's Word and the Holy Spirit. Satan's counterfeits actually open a person to demonic activity (2

Corinthians 11:13-15). Similar to asceticism and worshipping angels, the insistence on these visions eliminated the need for Jesus. Hebrews 4:14-16 encourages us to come boldly before the throne of grace, into God's presence directly because of Jesus. We don't need some other experience, vision or religious leader to do that.

These false practices were motivated by a heart that is puffed up without reason and a sensuous mind. The practices were rooted in spiritual pride whereas a true believer rooted in Jesus' finished work is humble, grateful and submissive. This spiritual pride was characterized by lacking even a basis for the pride. What the false teachers were insisting on had no value; it was empty. This baseless, worthless spiritual pride was actually the result of a sensuous mind or an unregenerate mind (Ephesians 4:17-19). Believers' minds have been regenerated, transformed and renewed. We are new creations. We have no part with anything related to our old, unregenerate selves. To seek God through any of these practices is idolatry. Jesus is our only means to God.

Paul explicitly informs believers who the true foundation of all things is—Jesus, 'the Head, from whom the whole body, nourished and knit together…grows…" Jesus, as the Head of the church, the body, is where we get our nourishment, all that we need to grow. He further clarifies that this growth is from God not certain practices or observances, not from worshipping angels or having visions. He emphasizes that these false practices and those behind them are not holding fast to Jesus. They are relying on their own works.

In contrast, the body of Christ is nourished as we spend time in fellowship with God (prayer), read and meditate on His Word and join in corporate worship and fellowship with other believers (knit together). Then God will grow us individually and as a body. There is nothing apart from God that we need for salvation or sanctification (growth).

For Reflection: On Day 16 we reflected on any areas we were living by Jesus + _____ (a human tradition or requirement). Today think if there are people that you are insisting on a human tradition or requirement for them to meet your standard of approval. If there are, first look at your own heart and the motivation behind it. Is it self-righteousness? Is it from your own guilt, so you seek to make someone else fall short? I encourage you to talk to the person(s) and ask forgiveness for seeking to impose legalism on them. Pray together. I know it can be scary, but it can also open the doors for being knit together and growing together.

Along the same lines as Jesus plus _____, think about where you might need to do a trust transfer. Sometimes thinking from a different angle will bring other areas to mind where we are looking to something or someone other than Jesus for our righteousness.

DAY 20

COLOSSIANS 2:20-23

If with Christ you died to the elemental spirits of the world,
why, as if you were still alive in the world, do you submit
to regulations—"Do not handle, Do not taste, Do not touch"
(referring to things that all perish as they are used)—according to
human precepts and teachings? These have indeed an appearance
of wisdom in promoting self-made religion and asceticism
and severity to the body, but they are of no value in stopping
the indulgence of the flesh.

If you met me today, you might notice that I tend to wear looser clothes. I do this in part because of a nerve sensitivity (I can't have too much pressure against my skin), but as some of you may have experienced, the older I get the easier it is for the pound here or there to hang on for dear life. Comfortable clothes are well, comfortable. However, when I was younger, thinner, vainer and yes, dumber, I would lie on my bed or the floor to get just enough extra tummy flatness to zip up those tight jeans. I can't even imagine how I walked or breathed in them. Now that I have experienced the freedom of properly fitting or looser clothing, I can't imagine going back. Why would I want to endure something so unnecessary and painful? Of course, there is other rationale for not going back (sinful fear of man, pride, etc.), but the freedom for my skin to breathe is a big one.

Paul addresses something similar in Galatians 5. "For freedom, Christ has set us free; stand firm therefore, and do not submit again to a yoke of slavery" (verse 1). This echoes what Paul has been teaching the Colossian believers and us the past few days. In today's verses, Paul restates what he has already said. He wants to drive this point home because it is so critical to the truth of the sufficiency of Jesus' atoning work and our position in Christ.

"If with Christ you died…" Paul does not use if as a conditional clause. He is writing to believers. They have died with Christ, but Paul instead is reminding them of their position (2:11-15). Since, the old self has died, why would they submit to the things of the old nature? Why would they return to works? Why would they do a reverse trust transfer?

In verse 22 Paul elaborates on the food and drink from verse 16 by defining them as perishable. The practices the false teachers insisted on held no eternal value. When you eat and drink, the food and drink are effectively destroyed. They end. Things of this world will all pass away. Adherence to and trust in man's traditions and regulations will not make us righteous. Only Christ can do that.

Legalism and asceticism have an appearance of wisdom. This mirrors the plausible arguments (verse 4) and deceitfulness of philosophy and human tradition (verse 8). However, as wise or pious as legalism and asceticism may seem, "they are of no value in stopping the indulgence of the flesh." Man's regulations are aimed at outward behavior not at the heart.

Warren Wiersbe depicts it this way, "The power of Christ in the life of the believer does more than merely restrain the desires of the flesh. It puts new desires within him."[33] This is the distinction between man's outward self-discipline and the self-control that results from the inward work of the Holy Spirit (Galatians 5:22-25). If the heart is not changed, if we only put off the sin but do not put on the godly response by the enabling of the Spirit, we will return to indulging the flesh.

I think David Guzik sums up chapter 2 beautifully. "Self-imposed religion is man reaching to God, trying to justify himself by keeping a list of rules. Christianity [the gospel] is God reaching down to man in love through Christ."[34]

For Reflection: "Some say He's keeping score, so try hard then try a little more. But hold up, if this were true, explain to me what the cross is for. So won't you come. Come all you weary and you burdened, you heavy ladened and you hurting, for all you with nothing left, come and find rest." (MercyMe, "Best News Ever").

With confidence go before the throne of grace. Pour out to the Father your burdens, your strivings and your own works apart from Jesus. Receive the mercy, grace, rest and peace that you need and that the Father longs to bestow on you. The works has already been done!

DAY 21

COLOSSIANS 3:1-2

*If then you have been raised with Christ, seek the things
that are above, where Christ is, seated at the right hand of God. Set
your minds on things that are above, not on things that are on earth.*

Ever since I was very young, I have enjoyed puzzles and mysteries. I have all the original Nancy Drew books including many first editions (thanks to my husband). Scooby Doo was my favorite cartoon (still is). I enjoy solving mysteries. An egg hunt is a type of mystery not only in finding the hidden eggs but in trying to think the way the hiders think. I was eight or nine years old when my uncle, aunt and two cousins visited for Easter. My Uncle Larry and Aunt Coral were both creative and mischievous. I am positive they helped hide the eggs that year because it was the most challenging hunt we ever had. I remember one egg in particular. I can still hear my Uncle saying look up. An egg was taped above the outside of the front door.

Usually the eggs, at least in my family, were hid closer to ground level. That's where I kept my eyes, but in this case, I needed to look up to find the prize.

Just as I was focused solely on what was at eye level or below, believers can get focused on the things of this world. We forget who God is and our identity in Christ, and then our perspective is shifted from an eternal viewpoint to a temporal, human viewpoint. This shift colors our thinking, emotions and actions. We are more prone to be discouraged, question the character of God in trials and live for what makes us happy right now. We'll try to do things in our own strength and wisdom. Our object of focus is essential.

Paul's typical format in writing is to lead in the first several chapters with what God has done for us in Christ and who we are in Christ. These are called indicatives. In our Colossians' study, some of the indicatives are Jesus' sufficiency and preeminence, Jesus' full deity and humanity, God has delivered us from the domain of darkness through Jesus' atoning death and resurrection (1:13), we find all wisdom in the person of Jesus (2:3), we are filled in Jesus (2:10), we have been buried, raised and made alive with Jesus (2:12-13), Jesus has cancelled the record of debt that was against us, and He has disarmed and shamed rulers and authorities. Whew! I don't know about you, but I need those reminders of God's lavished goodness, grace and mercy.

Just as in verse 2:20, Paul begins with *if* which might better be translated as *since*. This *is* our position in Christ. Not only have we been raised with Him now, made alive as new creations and children of God, but we will be raised experientially at the rapture and be glorified with Him (1 Corinthians 15:12-58). Verse 1 recalls what Paul taught us in chapters 1 and 2, the indicatives, and now transitions us to the imperatives—commands for us to obey with gratefulness and love because of what God has already done, continues to do and will do.

The first imperative or command that Paul gives us is to "seek the things above". To seek is to set our attention or direct our minds fully to searching out something. In verse 2, Paul reiterates this by calling the Colossian believers to "set your minds". It is a frame of mind, a mentality like a compass pointing us always to God and the things of God.

What exactly does it mean to set our minds on *things above*? Do we picture clouds, the throne or our future mansion? Certainly, directing our minds to eternity with God gives us hope now. It helps us persevere with joy knowing an eternity devoid of tears, death or pain awaits us as well as perfect fellowship with God. Paul does have in mind our future glorification (verse 4), but I think he also has a broader picture in mind. As we set our minds on things above, we make a deliberate choice to seek God Himself, to know Him more fully and to discern His will through prayer, His Word and the Holy Spirit's work in us.

As an example, let's examine the Israelites at the border of the Promised Land. God directed Moses to send twelve spies to survey Canaan and report back. Ten came back terrified. They saw the promised goodness of the land, but they also witnessed fortified cities and numerous, strong, gigantic people who devoured the inhabitants of the land. Their minds were set on earthly things to the extent of weeping and wishing they had died in Egypt or the wilderness. Can you envision what an earthly mindset leads to?

In contrast, Caleb and Joshua came back ready to occupy the land, "for we are able to overcome it...If the Lord delights in us, He will bring us into this land and give it to us, a land that flows with milk and honey. Only do not rebel against the Lord. And do not fear the people of the land, for they are bread for us. Their protection is removed from them, and the Lord is with us; do not fear them." Caleb and Joshua's minds were set on things above. Their minds were focused on their omnipotent, sovereign God who keeps His promises. The ten spies saw themselves as insignificant grasshoppers in comparison to the people of the land. Caleb and Joshua saw the people of the land as inconsequential grasshoppers in comparison to God (Numbers 13:25-14:9).

Caleb and Joshua first set their minds on things above and then viewed their circumstances through the lens of God's perspective. It was a completely opposite view from the earthly perspective of the ten spies and the rest of the Israelites who listened to them. Unfortunately for the Israelites, their earthly focus resulted in additional desert wandering until all those who doubted had died. None who listened to the ten spies entered the Promised Land (Numbers 14:20-24).

Before we end today, we will look at one more phrase, "where Christ is, seated at the right hand of God." To be seated to the right of a king was a place of honor (Psalm 45:9; 110:1). It is a position that highlights Jesus' sovereign rule. It is a position from which Jesus is a continual blessing to believers.

For Reflection: What earthly things do you tend to set your mind on? Are you fearing man or circumstances rather than God? What results of this do you observe in your life? Worry? Discouragement? Lack of obedience?

What truths do you need to set your mind on? What attributes of God would be encouraging to remember? What certainties of your position in Christ alter your perspective?

DAY 22

COLOSSIANS 3:3-4

*For you have died, and your life is hidden
with Christ in God. When Christ who is your life appears,
then you also will appear with Him in glory.*

I am from San Diego, but I married a Montana boy. We live in the Rocky Mountain part of Montana where there is plenty of wildlife. Often as we drive, we try to pick out deer or elk on the hillside. During winter that can be easier as they stand out more against the snowy backdrop, but around July, the hills start drying out and turn from green to shades of tan. The deer having similar coloring can seemingly disappear unless you catch their movement or have a really keen eye. You may have seen other animals camouflaged in nature.

Paul again reminds us that we have died with Christ. As we learned going through Colossians 2, our old nature was crucified Christ. It was put to death. It no longer has control over us. I like the picture Paul paints from 3:1 yesterday of Jesus at the right hand of God, sovereignly reigning. Sin doesn't rule us now. Before we died to our old nature, we were more like a deer or a black bear in winter starkly standing out against the snowy white. But now, raised to new life with Jesus, we are hidden with Him in God.

Positionally we are righteous because of Jesus' imputed righteousness to us. In Jesus we stand before God righteous, justified and glorified right now (Romans 8:30). This is called positional, declarative or definitive sanctification. It is how God sees us here and now because we are hidden with Christ in God, and God will complete the work He has begun in us (Philippians 1:6).

But, if you are anything like me, you know that day-to-day you still struggle with sin. Even Paul grieved that he didn't do the good he wanted to and did do the evil he didn't want to do (Romans 7:19). We are still in process of becoming what positionally we already are. Theologians call this progressive sanctification. This side of glory we by the Spirit move ever forward to conforming to the image of Jesus. Part of this process is putting off the practices of the old sin nature and putting on what belongs to the new self, the things that look more and more like Jesus, the things that are from above and not the earth (3:5 - 4:6)

Hidden is to conceal by covering. It's like a kept secret. During hunting season, I'm sure the deer are hoping they are covered and kept secret, but more beautiful is the picture of Jesus concealing us as our life is with Him in God. Like a hen tucking her chicks under her wing, we are safe and have joy and peace. We are satisfied. Jesus made the way for us to be children of God. With Christ in God there is nothing and no one that can ever separate us from the love of our Father (Romans 8:38-39).

I've been studying and teaching through Romans. In Romans 4:11 Paul describes the sign of circumcision as a seal of the righteousness Abraham received by faith. R.C. Sproul's comments connect with the word *hidden* in our study today.

"We, whose righteousness is as filthy rags, receive a new set of clothes, the clothing of the righteousness of Jesus, which is given to us as a *covering*. That is the gospel. This was dramatized constantly in the tabernacle and then in the temple of Israel. On the Day of Atonement when the animal was slain and his blood was carried into the Holy of Holies, the blood was sprinkled on the mercy seat. The blood was a covering on the throne of God. Habakkuk tells us that God is too righteous to even look at evil (Habakkuk 1:13), so unless we are covered, He will avert His glance from us. He will never make His face to shine upon us. He will never lift up the light of His countenance on us unless we are covered, and the only adequate covering that enables us to stand in His presence is the covering of the righteousness of Christ."[35]

The evil that our righteous God cannot look at was put to death in Jesus' atoning death (Colossians 2:12). We have been raised with Jesus to new life, with the new clothes of Jesus' righteousness covering us.

Jesus is described as being our life. 1 John 5:12 tells us, "Whoever has the Son has life; whoever does not have the Son of God does not have life." To Paul, to live was Christ and to die was gain (Philippians 1:21). "Eternal life is Jesus Christ Himself."[36] We are forever joined with Jesus never to be separated. Our future eternal life in glory is secure in Jesus.

Paul encourages us by pointing to our future hope. Jesus will return in the rapture for all that are in Him and take them to glory or heaven (1 Thessalonians 4:13-18). We will have glorified bodies, and all that was positionally true before will now be fully complete.

For Reflection: How does your life being hidden with Christ in God encourage you? Think about both your positional sanctification as well as your progressive sanctification.

How does your future appearing with Jesus in glory encourage and give you hope now?

DAY 23

COLOSSIANS 3:5-7

Put to death therefore what is earthly in you: sexual immorality,
impurity, passion, evil desire, and covetousness, which is idolatry.
On account of these the wrath of God is coming.
In these you too once walked, when you were living in them.

In my early twenties, a guy I worked with assaulted me. Although I spent time in prayer every day asking God to take away the dirty feelings, I also chose bulimia as my own way of ridding myself of the yuckiness. A common school of thought then and now is "once a bulimic, always a bulimic." You may be more familiar with that phrase being applied to an alcoholic or an addict. It left me feeling hopeless, and that I was in a losing battle. This is why one of my favorite verses when I counsel is 1 Corinthians 6:11. "And such *were* some of you. But you were washed, you were sanctified, you were justified in the name of the Lord Jesus Christ and by the Spirit of our God" (emphasis added).

1 Corinthians 6:11 parallels much of Colossians 2 and 3. In Colossians 3:7, we read, "once walked, when you were living in them." In both Colossians and 1 Corinthians, the past tense is used. This is who we *were*. It is not our identity anymore. The list we will look at today and tomorrow is what was buried with Jesus in His atoning death. In Colossians we determined that we have been made alive with Jesus (2:13, 20). Our sin nature no longer controls us. The penalty for sin has been paid on our behalf. We have a new nature. A new identity in Jesus with His righteous record imputed to us. Hope abounds in both the 1 Corinthians and Colossian verses. Human, plausible argument would inform me I am forever a bulimic. God's truth affirms that I am washed, sanctified, justified, a new creation, a child of God and no longer a slave to sin (in my case bulimia) but a slave to righteousness. That is true for every believer.

It is the most encouraging news we can hear because temptation still lurks and we often still choose to sin. Positionally we have Jesus' righteous record, our eternity with God is secure, but this side of eternal life, we continue to struggle with sin. So, Paul instructs us to "put to death therefore what is earthly in you".

Therefore is in the midst of the sentence, but it is crucial that we apply what it is referring back to first (verses 1-4). It can easily be discouraging or a trust transfer back to works if we neglect the *therefore*. Paul is reminding us to *be* what we already *are*. We aren't in a losing battle. Through the work of the Holy Spirit, we are more than conquerors (Romans 8:37). As a new creation in Christ, we can now choose the thing that glorifies God. We do not have to choose sin (1 Corinthians 10:13). The Holy Spirit indwells believers. We are not alone in this sanctification process. Knowing our identity in Christ and how God has equipped us, frees us to choose a righteous response out of love, gratitude, confidence and hope.

"Put to death" is one Greek word *nekroō*. It carries more punch than our English translation. Literally it means "to make dead". We are not to simply try to keep a certain sin under control or stuff it down. We are to do everything we can by the Spirit's power to exterminate the sin, wipe it out completely. I loathe snakes. Even glimpsing one on TV can give me nightmares. If I knew there was a snake in my house, there is nothing short of burning down the house that I wouldn't do to get rid of it. Casting it outside the door wouldn't be sufficient either. That snake would be as dead as a snake can be and probably thrown into the fire pit.

Paul specifically names specific sins to put off. "It is far easier to drift into a sin which one does not know by name than consciously to choose one whose very title should be repugnant to a Christian."[37] Knowing there was a critter in the house is one thing. Most critters I would just relocate them if I found them. I wouldn't necessarily even go on a hunt right then and there, but if you name a snake, Operation Take Down (as Katie Orr puts it) is in full force immediately. I will not sleep or eat until the snake is dead, Dead, DEAD! That is how Paul commands us to put to death what is earthly in ourselves.

Paul begins the put-to-death list with sexual immorality. This covers all types of sexual sins such as adultery, fornication, prostitution and every type of prohibited sex (Paul does get more specific in other letters). Roman society practiced everything imaginable. For anyone who thinks, "No problem here," recall Jesus' words in Matthew 5:27-28, "You have heard that it was said, 'You shall not commit adultery.' But I say to you that everyone who looks at a woman with lustful intent has already committed adultery with her in his heart." This is precisely what Paul classifies as *impurity*. It includes both sexual thoughts and intentions (1 Thessalonians 2:3-4).

Next on the hit list is *passion*. The Greek word *pathos* could be used for a good or a bad passion. In the New Testament it was used for depraved passions or inordinate (excessive) lust (1 Thessalonians 4:4-7). It can be sexual, but any sinful longing that drives us away from God needs to be put to death.

Paul is careful to describe what kind of desire is to be put to death. Desire or *epithymia* is a strong longing that again could be good. He used the same word in Philippians 1:23 to describe the great longing he had to see the Philippian believers. But in Colossians he qualifies it with the word *evil*—wicked, base, destructive and depraved. It can be connected to sexual sin as well. Paul is covering multiple facets of sexual sins with these first four because he knows they can be hard to resist especially as prevalent as it was in his day and currently in our culture. The reassurance Paul gives us in this battle is that they can be put to death. He wouldn't command the Colossian believers to do it if it were not possible with the aid of the Spirit.

Covetousness literally translates as "to have more"—a desire to get more, especially something forbidden, that can't be satisfied (Deuteronomy 5:21; James 4:2). Paul elaborates with "which is idolatry." Covetousness or any of the previous four sins places that desire ahead of desire for God and the things of God. That person worships themselves not God.

"We all have things, people, and desires we put before God. That's an idol, anything we want more than we want God. These idols can be good things, good people. Our friends. Our kids. Our job. Even our pursuits of God. Idolatry comes easily, and yet it often goes unrecognized in our lives."[38]

Paul takes a break in naming sins to interject, "On account of these the wrath of God is coming". These sins reflect how the world lives. We still have a choice whether we are going to identify with the world or put to death these sins and live according to who we are and to Whom we belong. God is holy and righteous. His righteous wrath demands judgment and punishment. Jesus took the Father's wrath, judgment and punishment on behalf of believers. For those who have not come to saving faith, God's wrath will come.

As we talked about in the beginning today, these sins are where we once walked, where we used to live. It is not our identity now, and as children of God, we cannot remain content with habitual, unrepentant sin. Yes, we will sin, but our sin will be like a snake in my house—detestable. It is an intruder that must go.

For Reflection: First, spend time thanking God for your identity in Christ. Express your gratitude that you are not what you once were.

Second, I was finding my identity in being a bulimic. Which sin, experience, or failing are you allowing to define you? How would you fill in the blank, "Once a _____ always a _____ (i.e., angry person, divorcee, abuse victim, gossip, single-parent, addict, laid off from a job, etc.).

Third, consider what things consume you. Are you more concerned with fellowship with God, God's plans and purposes or your own? Are you looking to others for praise, value and acceptance (fear of man)? Are you expecting circumstances or your accomplishments to satisfy you? Identify those areas. Confess them to God, and then rejoice in His forgiveness and Jesus' perfect, righteous record of worshipping God alone that is given to you.

DAY 24

COLOSSIANS 3:8-9

But now you must put them all away: anger, wrath, malice, slander, and obscene talk from your mouth. Do not lie to one another, seeing that you have put off the old self with its practices...

Don't be fooled by Paul's softer language in verse 8. We are not done eradicating snakes. Paul exposes more sinful heart issues for us. As we work through the list of sins today, notice a progression and connection between them—they originate inward and escalate outward. For many they have become acceptable. According to Warren Wiersbe, "We are so accustomed to anger, critical attitudes, lying, and coarse humor among believers that we are no longer upset or convicted about these sins. We would be shocked to see a church member commit some sensual sin, but we will watch him lose his temper in a business meeting and call it a 'righteous indignation.' "[39]

I appreciate that Paul recalls our new status—"seeing that you have put off the old self with its practices" and in verse 10 tomorrow that we "have put on the new self". He must know that naming all these sins can be discouraging. We need the repeated incentive of our new standing in Christ.

"Put them all away" and "put off the old self" illustrate the disposal of worn out, old clothes or in particular graveclothes. That is encouraging as we work through the sin to put off. Knowing that these sin practices are useless and belong in the casket might boost our efforts to put them to death. Who would want to walk around wrapped up in graveclothes?

We often use the word *anger* in English to describe a variety of anger-rooted responses. Paul uses three different words—anger, wrath and malice. *Anger* in the Greek is *orgē*. It is the opposite of agape (love that is unconditional and sacrificial). Anger has an element of habit to it, i.e., it can characterize a person. John MacArthur calls anger "a settled heart attitude."[40]

Wrath or *thymos* reminds me of a volcano that erupts. It may start with anger that is simmering down in the cauldron, but when anger isn't put off, it boils up suddenly, explodes and then subsides. This wrath is not to be confused with God's wrath or righteous anger. Our anger is rarely righteous (anger that someone has sinned against God). We are usually more concerned with how someone has sinned against us.

Malice is anger at another level. The Greek *kakia* is a term for general moral evil. It is a depravity that is not embarrassed about breaking laws. In our verse's context, it likely indicates the damage evil speech causes (1 Peter 2:1). It is someone who does a happy dance when you fail and is dismal when you succeed.

Slander is frequently translated as *blasphemy* (KJV) and generally refers to sacrilegious speech against God. In our context, it is better understood as a blasphemy against another person. It injures a person's good reputation.

Obscene talk is foul or filthy communication. It can include coarse humor. We will study Colossians 4:6 in depth later, but for now, it says, "Let your speech always be gracious, seasoned with salt, so that you may know how you ought to answer each person." Well-seasoned speech is a glaring disparity to the types of anger and speech we have examined.

Lastly, Paul charges us not to lie to one another. Actually, in the Greek, it reads more like, "Stop lying!" Lying is any intent to deceive or misrepresent the truth. Our words can even be accurate, but it is a lie if the motive is deception. There is no such thing as a little, white lie. That is merely a way to make a lie seem acceptable. Satan is the father of lies (John 8:44), so lying cooperates with him. That should make lying vile to us.

Are we done yet? That was a depressing list of things to put off. Likely there were more things in this second part of Paul's list that we recognize in ourselves. There is a reason James describes the tongue guiding the whole body or starting a forest fire. "How great a forest is set ablaze by such a small fire! And the tongue is a fire, a world of unrighteousness. The tongue is set among our members, staining the whole body, setting on fire the entire course of life, and set on fire by hell…From the same mouth come blessing and cursing. My brothers, these things ought not to be so" (James 3:36, 10).

I want to end today with a reassuring prayer from Katie Orr. "God, I praise You that even when I was dead in my nasty transgressions, You came to rescue me. Thank You for drawing me up from the pit, out of the deep mess I was in. I confess that I keep returning to that mess. Something about it is comfortable and gratifying, but I know it only brings destruction to me and those around me. Most importantly, it draws me away from You. Holy Spirit, help me to walk away from the sin that so easily entangles me. Show me what it looks like for me to lay it aside today. I am desperate for the change that only You can bring. I praise You for Your great, great, glorious grace."[41]

For Reflection: If you would like further guidance in putting off anger or putting off sin in general, *Anger: Calming Your Heart (31-Day Devotionals for Life)* by Robert D. Jones[42] and *Everyday Obedience* (devotional) by Katie Orr[43] are both excellent.

Which of today's sins do you struggle with most? Tomorrow we will begin to look at the godly responses we replace sins with, but for today name specifically what you need to put off. Take hope that God enables you to do it. He has not abandoned you to face it alone. There is also reason for thanksgiving that these sins of our tongue are no longer our identity. Every day is a day to thank God for Jesus' righteousness given to us.

DAY 25

COLOSSIANS 3:10-11

And have put on the new self, which is being renewed
in knowledge after the image of its Creator. Here there
is not Greek and Jew, circumcised and uncircumcised, barbarian,
Scythian, slave, free; but Christ is all, and in all.

I know this isn't true for all women, but in general women like getting new clothes and shoes. When we are little, we play dress up. As we get older, we like to find the perfect outfit for work or a fancy night out. We search for shoes that are not just the right color but the right style for an outfit. Clothes can make us feel beautiful and confident. I have a pair of knee-high white boots with bling buckles on the side that make me feel fun and maybe a wee sassy.

Before anyone goes on the offensive, I am not advocating for finding our identity in how we look or judging ourselves or others by the clothes we wear. However, clothes can make us feel different.

Even guys seem to be more in fan-mode when they wear their favorite football jersey. If we can feel this way towards fabric, how incredibly much more should we delight in putting on our dazzling new righteous wardrobe that Jesus paid for with His life? Unlike the physical clothes we wear that only change our outward appearance, the godly responses we put on are a result of a changed heart.

All we had to wear before the Father was our filthy, sinful graveclothes. Jesus by his death and resurrection has purchased an incorruptible wardrobe for us. I am still processing the Greek nuances here, but the short version is that "do not lie" (verse 9) is the main verb. The "put off" that follows it and the "put on" in verse 10 are participles connected to the main verb. Lying is part of the old self. It does not go with the new self. The new self has a whole new wardrobe from Jesus.

For those not fond of clothes shopping, Jesus has filled our closet with everything we ever need for every occasion for life and godliness (2 Peter 1:3). In the next couple of days, we will behold part of our closet—compassion, kindness, humility, meekness, patience, forgiveness, and love. Our closet also includes the whole armor of God (Ephesians 6:11-17) and the fruit of the Spirit (Galatians 5:22-23). We are decked out with the entirety of our new self and all paid for and provided by Jesus. Our part is to put it on daily (progressive sanctification from Day 22).

Our new self is being *renewed*, meaning we are continuously being renewed. We have been transformed to a new life that is in total opposition to our previous corrupt state (Romans 12:2; Ephesians 4:22-24). We are in process of becoming what we already are positionally (progressive sanctification again).

How does this renewing happen? We are renewed "in knowledge after the image of its creator." The more we know God and choose our new clothes in Christ, the more we become like Christ our Creator (Romans 8:29; 1 Corinthians 15:49). Adam was created in the image of God (Genesis 1:27), but then he sinned. His nature was corrupted resulting in everyone after him being born in sin. Jesus as the second Adam (1 Corinthians 15:20-28, 45-49) conforms believers more and more to His image (progressive sanctification) which will be complete on the day of Jesus' return (Philippians 1:6). If you study the clothes we are to put on, they "can be traced to the character of God generally, or to Christ specifically. This demonstrates how literally Paul understood the idea of believers taking on the 'image' of their Creator."[44]

Before Paul moves on to what we put on as "God's chosen ones, holy and beloved," he brings us back to 1:27 and the wonderful truth that the gospel is for the Gentiles too. Paul elaborates on this because the culture had so many divisions. Greeks and Jews didn't get along. Greeks thought their culture was superior. Jewish believers wanted Greeks to adhere to their ceremonial laws like circumcision. Compared to Jewish ceremonial laws, many of the Greek foods, customs and beliefs were taboo. Barbarians didn't speak Greek, so were considered uncivilized by the Greeks. Scythians came from modern day Russia. They were deemed savages like wild beasts, nomadic and seeking war. In the Roman class system, slaves were regarded as subhuman.

Racism and social barriers were rampant. This environment would have everyone looking at Paul's list of put offs and self-righteously pointing the finger at all the others because they were inferior. The list probably reaffirmed in their minds their perception of the others, so Paul clarifies the matter in no uncertain terms, "but Christ is all, and in all." That Jesus is all reminded the Colossian believers and us of Jesus' preeminence (1:18). That He is in all makes it abundantly clear that Jesus is the all-sufficient Lord and Savior equally to everyone. In Galatians, Paul applies it to the equal standing of both men and women before God (3:28). James applies it to favoritism of the rich (James 2:1-9). Discrimination for any reason in the church is unbiblical.

Verse 11 is also an admonition of our need for the church body. Christianity isn't a solo act. It isn't a quartet with only those whom we beautifully harmonize. The Trinity exemplifies fellowship. God created us for fellowship with Him and with other believers (3:15).

For Reflection: Often we can be weighed down with the sin we still see in our lives and be blind to how God has been sanctifying us. Think back over time and discover ways God has been conforming you to the image of His Son. God has been working. He is working. He will continue working in you. Those changes are cause for thankfulness and encouragement as we daily choose to put off the old sin clothes and put on our new righteous clothes.

All forms of discrimination still exist in the church. How have you been tempted to discriminate? Is there anyone you have viewed as being unequal to yourself? Do you think there are others less deserving of the grace God gives you? There is lavish grace for this too. Confess any discrimination to God and to the person if that is fitting. In Christ, today is a new day for you to extend the grace you have been given and put off any biases.

DAY 26

COLOSSIANS 3:12-13

Put on then, as God's chosen ones, holy and beloved, compassion, kindness, humility, meekness, and patience, bearing with one another and, if one has a complaint against another, forgiving each other; as the Lord has forgiven you, so you also must forgive.

By now, you understand the concept of putting off and putting on being likened to clothes. I love how God through Paul encourages us one more time before we go to the "put on" commands. Robert D. Jones in his devotional *Anger: Calming Your Heart* illustrated our verses with the following diagram.

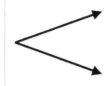

Who You Are
Chosen, Holy,
Loved, Forgiven

What You Should Be
Compassionate, Kind,
Humble, Gentle, Patient

What You Should Do
Bear With, Forgive, Love

Paul says first that we are chosen ones. We do not come to saving faith exclusively on our own. Romans 8:30 describes God's action on our behalf to which we respond in faith. "And those whom He pre-destined [chose] He also called, and those whom He called He also justified, and those whom He justified He also glorified." He chose us for the purpose of being conformed to the image of His Son (verse 29). Being chosen resonates with me, as I was twice adopted. My parents chose me as a baby to adopt into their family for which I will be forever grateful. God chose me to be His child too. I am even more thankful to be in God's family where I am being made more like Jesus.

Second, we are holy. God has set us apart from the world and to Himself. We are His children and His witnesses. Third, we are beloved. When God in love chose us (Ephesians 1:4-5), we became the recipients of His great love (1 John 3:1a). God loved us so much that He sent His Son to be our atonement (John 3:16). Love is one of our primary motivations to obey God.

Fourth, we are forgiven. We have been forgiven by God for far greater sin than anyone could ever sin against us (Matthew 18:21-35). Not only are we forgiven, but Jesus willingly sacrificed His own life as payment for our sin so that we could be forgiven. In addition, God has removed our sins as far as the east is from the west (Psalm 103:12). He chooses not to remember them against us. Gratitude for the forgiveness we have received is our second motivation for obedience and forgiving others.

Bolstered by who we are in Christ, we are able by the Spirit to put on the actions and attitudes that glorify and reflect God. Compassion may be translated as "tender mercies". It is a heart (bowels in the KJV) tenderness that is reflected in outward good towards others. A compassionate person can feel the smallest amount of another's misery.

Kindness is a moral goodness or integrity towards another that is pervasive. It is a fruit of the Spirit. In the Old Testament kindness was used "for expressing the abundance of His goodness which He displays to His covenant people—indeed to all men as His creatures. His constant mercy and readiness to help are essential themes of the Psalms as well as in the prophets where the kindness of God is all the more amazing in the face of His people's sin."[45] An example of kindness is found in the parable of the Good Samaritan (Luke 10:25-37). Samaritans and Jews did not associate, but it was the Samaritan alone who stopped to help the Jewish man who was beaten, robbed and left for dead. The Samaritan got the man to safety and paid out of his own money for the man to be cared for. This is kindness.

The Greeks despised humility. They valued pride and domination which in the Old Testament were often contrasted with humility and were marked for judgment (Proverbs 11:2; 16:18; Amos 2:6-7; Isaiah 2:9, 11, 17). Paul wrote of Jesus' ultimate pattern of humility in Philippians 2:3-11. "who, though He was in the form of God, did not count equality with God a thing to be grasped, but made Himself nothing, taking the form of a servant, being born in the likeness of men. And being found in human form, He humbled Himself by becoming obedient to the point of death, even death on a cross" (verses 6-8). Humility for us is counting others as more significant than ourselves and looking to their interests as well as our own (verses 3-4). It does mean that we are a doormat to be trampled all over, but we, in love, choose to lift up others instead of promoting ourselves.

Meekness was considered a weakness during Paul's time, but that is not God's definition. Meekness is actually power that is under control like a calming wind that has the potential to be a horrific storm. It is a fruit of the Spirit (gentleness). A meek person trusts and rests in God's sovereignty instead of worrying about how they are treated. They are willing to be hurt or insulted rather than retaliate. A spirit of meekness is patterned after Jesus (Matthew 11:29; 2 Corinthians 10:1).

Patience or longsuffering endures the sins of others rather than responding in anger or seeking revenge. Jesus exemplified this during His trial and crucifixion. It is also a fruit of the Spirit.

We are to bear with one another. God forbears with us in holding back His judgment (Romans 2:4; 3:25). We bear with others when we hold them up or we hold back our condemnation of them. We endure with others. It flows from patience and is continual. Although I have sometimes wished that there was a limit on how long I must forbear, God does not put a time frame on forbearance.

As we touched on earlier, because of the great forgiveness God has given us, we are to forgive others. God in forgiving us chooses not to allow our sin to stand between us, not to dwell on our sin and not to use it against us. We are to follow God's example as well as not sharing someone's sin with others.

Often what we want to put on is diligence, competence, knowledge and whatever else the world considers individual success. Paul's list of graces is relational. They are between us and other people. They are how we conduct ourselves towards others. They are not for self-promotion.

For Reflection: Did any of these graces to put on stand out to you? Why? Which ones do you struggle with the most? Why? It's easy to say, "I'm just not a kind person," but as children belonging to God, these aren't an option. We need to look at what is really driving our struggle or rebellion, put that off, and choose to respond in the way that glorifies and reflects God.

DAY 27

COLOSSIANS 3:14-15

And above all these put on love, which binds everything together in perfect harmony. And let the peace of Christ rule in your hearts, to which indeed you were called in one body. And be thankful.

I love doing things for people. I love finding the perfect gift for someone. I love finding ways to bless others, but none of these necessarily equates to loving others or them feeling loved by me. Although love is an action not simply an emotion, real love, God's kind of love, springs from the right motivation. My motivation is often mixed. Yes, I do care about the people I do things for, but in addition there can be a desire for recognition and/or thinking I'm earning favor with God. Jesus said that our good works should cause others to glorify the Father not self (Matthew 5:16). Paul said that without love all my actions are a noisy gong, a clanging cymbal, and I am nothing.

Paul didn't stick love at the end of his "put ons" because it wasn't important. In Corinthians he calls it the greatest virtue (1 Corinthians 13:13). We know that God is love (1 John 4:8). Jesus stated that others would know we are His disciples by our love for one another. Love is crucial. The graces we looked at yesterday are all facets of love (1 Corinthians 13:4-8). None of them have real value if they are outward only and not from an inward motivating love.

Authentic love "binds everything together in perfect harmony." Love is like the ligaments that keep the parts of our body united together. It is an apt description since Paul calls the church a body with each person being a different part (1 Corinthians 12:12). No coincidence that Paul follows up his illustration of the church as a body with an exhortation on real love (1 Corinthians 13). He knows the body is comprised of sinners. We need God's love enabling us to show love to others.

"Perfect harmony" means completeness or perfection. Paul affirms that God continues to work progressive sanctification in us until we are complete (Philippians 1:6). *Complete* in Philippians is a form of the same Greek word for *perfect harmony*. The point is that we were not made to grow in sanctification on our own little island. God in His divine wisdom uses others to help us reach completeness, but it is possible only if we are loving others as God loves us.

Peace. Most of us desire peace. A peaceful home without children fighting or making demands. Peace at work so we accomplish our tasks. We long for world peace with no wars or peace within our own country. Believers frequently wait for a sign of peace to make a decision. This verse is often misused that way. God sometimes grants us peace in decision making, but that is not what Paul is exhorting. Peace is in the context of believers being called in one body. When possible, as far as it depends on us, we are to live at peace with all (Romans 12:18). We cover offenses in love (1 Peter 4:8). We forgive in love when it is not something we can overlook (Colossians 3:13). We seek peace as long as the matter does not require us to compromise the gospel. I understand there are reasons for different denominations, but it makes me sad that there are many ways we could still be at peace with other churches and work together for God's glory (like advocating for pro-life or caring for the homeless), but we let those differences keep us divided.

"And be thankful." A short sentence but poignant. I am a sinner. You are a sinner. We are sinners together in the body of Christ. We are both recipients of God's grace and mercy. My tendency is to focus on the sins of others instead of choosing to love, pursue peace and practice compassion, kindness, humility, meekness, patience, forbearance and forgiveness. However, when I pause, pray and consider the good God is working in others, their gifts, God's blessing of the body and His patience with sinful me, I am thankful. Thankfulness propels me beyond criticism to love.

For Reflection: Start with thanksgiving today especially thanksgiving for God's perfect, amazing, unmerited love lavished on you. Add to your thankful journal some specific ways He has shown His love to you.

Read 1 Corinthians 13 (it's not that long!). Meditate on each of the characteristics of love. Are there ways you love well when you look at the characteristics of love? Are there ways your love is lacking keeping in mind that your lack of loving doesn't change how God sees you with Jesus' perfect record of loving others? One that I have been working on is love "believes all things." Love chooses to believe the best about others instead of jumping to the worst (or at least not so favorable) conclusion. This is one where taking time to consider what I have to be thankful for in that person helps me to choose to believe the best about them instead of the worst.

Where is an area in your local church that you can pursue peace? Have you been avoiding someone that is different from you? Do you outright argue with someone who disagrees with you? Are you holding grudges? Is there something you need to overlook in love? Is there someone with whom you need to reconcile? Maybe it is supporting those in a ministry in which you are not involved (volunteer for a special event they do, pray with them, tell them you appreciate what they do).

How can you pursue peace with other churches? You can invite someone from another church to a special event at your church, go to one at theirs or organize a joint function. Perhaps another church has a ministry your church doesn't have that you could support like an outreach to the homeless or help for addicts. It could be as simple as praying for other churches or not looking down on them for understanding Scripture differently.

DAY 28

COLOSSIANS 3:16-17

*Let the word of Christ dwell in you richly, teaching
and admonishing one another in all wisdom, singing psalms and
hymns and spiritual songs, with thankfulness in your hearts to God.
And whatever you do, in word or deed, do everything in the name
of the Lord Jesus, giving thanks to God the Father through Him.*

My mom, her mom and at least one of her aunts were teachers. My other grandma was an elementary school secretary. When I was young, I remember vowing never to be a teacher. I'm not sure why. My Mom is a wonderful teacher. I think it had more to do with wanting my own identity than thinking teaching was bad. God has a sense of humor, though, because what I now enjoy is teaching - not math or English (I like both) and definitely not science, but God's Word. I like studying first, but then finding the right way to take the riches of God's truth and teach it in a way that it clicks in people's minds and hearts. I prefer teaching high schoolers, but really it is exciting to see any age grasp the truths in God's Word. It is even more thrilling when I see a person applying God's truth to their life and conform a bit more to the image of Jesus. It's one of my greatest joys as a youth leader.

As we approach today's verses you may be thinking that Paul is addressing pastors or seminary professors or my high school Bible teacher. I have good news for you. He isn't. Yes, it really is good news. He's addressing you and everyone else in the body of Christ. Verse 16 is still in the context of those who have been raised with Christ (3:1), God's chosen ones (3:12) and one body in Christ (3:15). Like Moses, you are coming up with excuses. He had several, but his last-ditch effort was, "Oh, my Lord, I am not eloquent, either in the past or since You have spoken to Your servant, but I am slow of speech and of tongue" (Exodus 4:10). God answers, "Who has made man's mouth? Who makes him mute, or deaf, or seeing, or blind? Is it not I, the Lord? Now therefore go, and I will be with your mouth and teach you what you shall speak (Exodus 4:10-12). Can you believe after God's answer that Moses again tried to squirm out of going back to Egypt? It didn't work. Moses went, and God provided His strength in Moses' weakness.

Even if you are biting your nails or pulling your hair over the idea of teaching, stick with me today. Closing this book or your Bible won't make the verse or the command disappear. How about we start with the part before the teaching—"Let the word of Christ dwell in you richly"?

"The Word," "The Word of God," or "The Word of the Lord" are other ways to refer to the Scriptures. Some commentators believe Paul used "the Word of Christ" as the person and work of Jesus is central to this letter, but Paul could have also used this term to specifically focus on the gospel to which Jesus is essential. All of

Scripture revolves around Jesus and His redemptive work, so we should meditate on it, but Paul additionally says that "all Scripture is breathed out by God and profitable for teaching, for reproof, for correction, and for training in righteousness, that the man of God may be competent, equipped for every good work" (2 Timothy 3:16-17). We have the entirety of Scripture at our fingertips which the Colossians did not. We can dwell on the whole of Scripture viewing it through the gospel message.

Dwell means to be at home. I realize home isn't the same for everyone, but in general it is the place we come back to every day, where we keep our clothes and our things, where we don't have a second thought about raiding the refrigerator or wearing our pjs until noon. It is our place. Paul combines *dwell* with *richly* or abundantly. Together these words instruct us that God's Word is to infiltrate every aspect of our lives. It will govern our thoughts, words and actions (Psalm 119:11; Philippians 2:16; 2 Timothy 2:15). It should be at home in us.

Paul David Tripp comments, "Ministry opportunities will tend to devolve into human advice giving. Because we don't know God's Word well, we will dip into our own experience and tell people what we think they should do, ignoring God's call to them, His grace in them, and His wisdom for them."[46]

One of the first things I learned when I was pursuing my Biblical counseling certification is that everyone counsels or teaches every day. You may not think of it that way, but when a co-worker is considering a job change, you give input or counsel. When friend rants about problems with her husband, you sympathize and offer your advice. One friend complains about another friend who has been blowing her off. You have something to say. All those responses are counsel; they are teaching what you believe. The question is whether it is rooted in God's Word or in human ability, mindset or experience.

We all teach, but Paul's charge is to let that teaching spring forth from God's Word indwelling you. Tied to that is another key principle in Biblical counseling that God's Word is sufficient for "all things that pertain to life and godliness" (2 Peter 1:3). We have what we need in God's Word to be able to teach others.

"It's clear here that he's [Paul] talking about the myriad of every-day-life ministry opportunities that God will give every one of His children. According to Paul, you have been called to teach. And if you want to understand what that means, you need to understand that there's no real separation between life and ministry. Rather, the Bible teaches that every dimension of human life is, at the very same time, a forum for ministry."[47]

Paul says we teach and admonish. Admonish is our same Greek word from Colossians 1:28 that was translated as warning—*noutheteō*. From Strong's Concordance, "(admonish through instruction) especially appeals to the mind, supplying doctrinal and spiritual substance (content). This 'exerts positive pressure' on someone's logic (reasoning), i.e. urging them to choose (turn to) God's best."

Teaching and admonishing are to be done "in all wisdom". Already in Colossians we have been learning the importance Paul put on gaining true wisdom and knowledge and Who the source is—"be filled with the knowledge of His will in all spiritual wisdom and understanding" (1:9); "increasing in the knowledge of God" (1:10); "teaching everyone with all wisdom" (1:28); "which is Christ, in whom are hidden all the treasures of wisdom and knowledge" (2:3). Wisdom and knowledge are not for hoarding or being puffed up, rather they enable us to help others in their sanctification, ultimately to God's glory.

Teaching and admonishing in the Greek grammar are tied to "singing psalms and hymns and spiritual songs" which we also see in Ephesians 5:19. This is reflective of corporate worship. Our worship is directed to God, but in corporate worship there is the element of edifying the body as well. This means that the singing is connected to the Word of Christ and wisdom. It serves as a caution for the lyrics that we choose in our worship. We should be diligent to sing only what is rooted in the truth of God's Word. And for those who are wondering, there really aren't any distinctions between psalms, hymns and spiritual songs. Most likely Paul is denoting variety not specific categories we must utilize in corporate worship.

As Paul commanded thankfulness in verse 15, he repeats it in verse 16. Thankfulness to God should characterize our lives and be reflected in our teaching, admonishing and singing. I have heard some teach or talk about God without any evidence of joy and gratitude to God. It makes me wonder what motivates them. They appear to be going through motions. Then I've listened to people who overflow with authentic love, gratitude and joy in God. It makes their message contagious. In verse 17, Paul reiterates giving thanks to the Father through Jesus. Are you getting the idea that Paul wants us to be thankful? That it is a crucial part of our sanctification? Thankfully, we will never run out of things to be thankful for as God conforms us to the image of His Son.

Paul wraps up this section instructing the Colossian believers that "whatever you do, in word or deed, do everything in the name of the Lord Jesus." In chapter 3, Paul taught through what we are to put off and put on as a result of our identity in Christ or how we are to act towards others particularly in the body of Christ. In 3:18-4:1, Paul will continue with instructions for how we are to live out our sanctification in specific relationships. In all these, we are to consistently conduct ourselves in alignment with who Jesus is and what He desires.

In Paul's time, a name held great importance. We bear Jesus' name. We are identified with Him. Our words and actions will bring glory to Him or will tarnish His name. Remembering that we are Jesus' representatives, and even more that we already have His righteous-ness will help us choose what honors Him.

I want to end today with one last quote from Paul David Tripp. "Personal ministry [teaching and admonishing] is not just about con-fronting people with principles, theology, or solutions. It confronts people with the God who is active and glorious in His grace and truth, and who has a rightful claim to our lives."[48] Sometimes when we immerse ourselves in God's Word, we forget that the goal is not just to spout the truth. God's Word is meant to always drive us to God in personal relationship.

For Reflection: As you thought about the Word of Christ dwell-ing in you, maybe you were discouraged. You don't feel like it does. Maybe devotions are a struggle. I think most believers go through tropical islands and deserts in their devotional time. That you have been persevering through this study is a good start. I have often prayed for God to give me a passion for Him and His Word. I don't always feel excited about my quiet times, or I get easily distracted. Ask God for help. He delights in time with you. He wants you to delight in your time together too.

Scripture memory and talking about what you are learning are ways to aid God's Word richly indwelling you.

Ask the Spirit to help you be aware in your conversations of whether you are teaching and admonishing from God's Word or from self. I've found that pausing, listening to the other person, and saying a quick prayer that I would speak from God's wisdom, helps me to be more purposeful in how I respond.

Don't be discouraged. This is all a process, and we are journey-ing through it together.

DAY 29

COLOSSIANS 3:18-21

*Wives, submit to your husbands, as is fitting in the Lord.
Husbands, love your wives, and do not be harsh with them. Children,
obey your parents in everything, for this pleases the Lord. Fathers,
do not provoke your children, lest they become discouraged.*

Today's verses may step on a few toes. The idea of submission has been taken to extremes in both directions resulting in hurt and division in families. I believe God's design for submission is good as I hope you will see today. We will discuss that submission in any relationship is not about inferiority. We see that reflected initially in Paul addressing wives, husbands, children, servants and masters as equals in the body of Christ. This was revolutionary at this time. Males had rights that wives, children and slaves did not. They could decide if their infants lived or died. Slaves were property like a piece of machinery. Wives weren't considered much better. Loving husbands were rare.

A beautiful pattern for submission has been set in the Trinity. They are three persons together in one being (one of those Biblical truths that we might not fully wrap our minds around until heaven). We could spend several days talking about the Trinity, but I will try to simplify it for our purposes. They are all unified and equally God (Colossians 1:19), but they have different roles in creation and redemption (theologians describe this as the economic Trinity). Although equal to the Father, Jesus willingly submitted to the Father's plan of redemption (Philippians 2:6-11; John 5:19-23). Jesus' submission to the Father's will doesn't diminish His deity in any way.

"As we walk with Christ in submission to Him (Romans 8:7), we have no problem submitting to one another and seeking to serve one another. But where there is selfishness, there will be conflict and division."[49]

When God created Adam and Eve, He made them in His image (Genesis 1:27). This means we were created for relationships just as the Father, Son and Holy Spirit are relational and unified. And like the Trinity, God designed different roles for men and women. It does not mean that women are inferior to men or vice versa. God is a God of order not chaos. Different roles even within the Trinity are part of creating order. It is also important to remember that in creating that first family, God was creating the foundation of society. He designed family a specific way with a specific purpose. When we mess with that, it affects all of society. We see the impact from broken homes alone.

So here it is... "wives, submit to your husbands, as is fitting in the Lord." Picture a chalkboard with the word submit and whatever definition you have for it written on the chalkboard. Now get an eraser and wipe it all away. Let's start with a clean slate. God's definition of submission is to willingly place yourself under someone or something. Read that again. This is not a forced action by the husband. It is not a begrudging action by the wife. It does not mean inferiority (Galatians 3:28). In fact, many women in the Old and New Testaments are held up as examples of godliness and usefulness in the church and to their husbands. God would not make the wife a helpmate to her husband if she did not have gifts, wisdom and abilities that could aid him.

Submission is a willing action by the wife to place herself under her husband's care and authority. Note the *your* before husbands. Women are not required to have this submission to all men in all situations.

If we reference Philippians 2:6-7 again, we observe Jesus' example. "Who, though He was in the form of God, did not count equality with God a thing to be grasped, but made *Himself* nothing, taking the form of a servant, being born in the likeness of men" (emphasis added). It goes on to say that Jesus was obedient even to the point of death on a cross. First, Jesus priority wasn't holding on to His equality. His priority was glorifying the Father and doing what was necessary for the bigger, redemption picture. Second, He made Himself nothing. The Father didn't force Jesus to do it. Jesus didn't do it kicking and screaming. He willingly chose to place Himself under the Father's good plan and purpose. In addition, Jesus submitted to His earthly parents (Luke 2:51).

To complete our definition, we need to look at the end of the instruction. We find the wife's motive—it is not her duty to her husband; it is her duty to God. It is what pleases God and brings Him glory. Wives are ultimately submitting to God, trusting Him, His faithfulness and provision as she submits to her husband.

There are a few more things relating to submission. We already stated that it does not mean inferiority. It does not give the husband permission to be a tyrant. It is not conditional on the husband fulfilling his role which is why Paul wrote, "as is fitting in the Lord." Finally, it is not absolute. A wife does not need to place herself under her husband if he is asking her to sin (in that case, God is the higher authority, Acts 5:29), if he is mentally incapacitated, if he is threatening the wife physically or has broken the marriage covenant by adultery.

Husbands are told to love their wives not to rule them. The Greek verb tense is a continuous action—"keep on loving". It is not based on passion or feeling. Just like the wife's submission, it is a willing choice. It models Jesus' selfless love for the church (Ephesians 5:25-33). Jesus gave His own life for the church that she might be holy and without blemish. Likewise, husbands in loving their wives, care for their needs and encourage their growth and gifts. 1 Corinthians 13 is a blueprint on what love looks like. David Guzik paraphrases it as, "Husband, continually practice self-denial for the sake of your wife."[50]

Husbands are further commanded not to be harsh with their wives. Harsh in the Greek is to be embittered against or to harbor bitterness (Ephesians 4:31; Hebrews 12:15). Bitterness is capable of contaminating the whole family not only the wife.

A husband and wife's first priority is to each other. God's design is that children leave the home eventually cleaving to their own spouse. Often parents prioritize the children to the neglect of the husband-wife relationship. Parents have a responsibility to care for and train up their children, but the best way to do that is by modeling a godly marriage to them and the proper priorities within the family, demonstrating their submission to the Lord and each other.

Paul transitions to commands to the children. The word *children* can embody any child that is currently living in their parents' home and under their authority. *Obey* is a command for continued obedience. Throughout life there are situations where we all must submit to or obey and respect an authority (i.e. a boss at a job). This begins in the home with children being taught to obey their parents. Paul says this obedience is "in everything." The only exception is if the child is being asked to sin. Similar to a wife's submission to her husband, children are to obey because it "pleases the Lord." A child's motivation in obedience is pleasing God, not staying out of trouble or from fear of man. Adult children do not fall under the command to obey, but they are still called to honor their parents (Ephesians 6:2).

Paul also addresses the parent relationship to the child. *Fathers* in Greek is *pateres* which is translated as parents in Hebrews 11:23. Fathers and mothers (although fathers may be in view here as the head of the household) are told not to provoke their children. To provoke means to stir up or exasperate possibly to anger as the King James adds. "Parents can provoke their children by being too harsh, too demanding (setting their child up to fail), too controlling, unforgiving, or just plain angry. This harshness can be expressed through words, through actions, or through non-verbal communication."[51] Children may also be used as weapons or put in the middle when parents are fighting.

Paul warns that provoking children can lead to their discouragement. It is like taking the wind out of a sail. They lose their courage and spirit. They can become listless, sullen or hopeless. Discouraged children can be more vulnerable to deceptive temptations. Although the child is still responsible for their choice, parents are responsible if they are setting them up for that temptation.

Instead of provoking their children, parents should listen to their children. In taking time to listen, you may discover more of your child's heart, understanding their feelings and frustrations which gives you better insight on how to encourage their spiritual growth. Parents should pray with their children and encourage them in their gifts and with the truth of God's Word. "A survey in one town indicated that fathers spent only thirty-seven seconds a day with their small sons."[52] What a sad statistic. God's design is for parents to be a child's principal source of learning. That requires parents spending quality time with their children.

For Reflection: You might be in a different stage of life then today's verses are talking about (single, widows, childless or an empty nester), but you can still apply these verses. Single women, you can cultivate a heart that is submissive to others (Philippians 2:3-8) that can help prepare you for submission to a future husband. Single men, you can cultivate loving others (1 Corinthians 13) especially in situations where you are an authority (job, ministry). Those without children usually have some teaching opportunities in ministry or with nieces and nephews. You can practice listening to children now. Widows and empty nesters can encourage and mentor wives, husbands and parents in living out these verses from the experience they have had.

If you are a wife or a woman, how does your view of submission align with the Biblical view? If you are a wife, do you need to ask God and your husband's forgiveness for not willingly placing yourself under your husband's care and authority? What are some specific ways you can submit yourself to your husband? Do you see this ultimately as something that pleases God?

If you are a man or a husband, how does your view of a husband's role and a wife's submission align with Scripture? If you are a husband, are there ways you have abused your authority that you need to seek God and your wife's forgiveness? What are some specific steps you can take in loving your wife, caring for her needs (spiritual, physical, emotional) and encouraging her growth and gifts?

Children, God does not leave any loopholes for you not to obey your parents whether you agree with them or not unless they are asking you to sin like lying to a teacher. It is His sovereign plan for your good to place them as your parents. You obey them because it pleases God. I understand, some of you may be in difficult homes where your parents may not be caring for and loving you as parents should. Obeying them is your opportunity to show them Jesus. You may be who God uses to change their lives.

Parents, are there ways you have been provoking your children? Do you need to ask God and their forgiveness? Admitting your sin is a wonderful way to model God's work in your life and foster an atmosphere for your children to come to you with their sin. As you seek to listen to, pray with and encourage your children, set aside some time each week or every couple of weeks with each child. Go for ice cream or do something together that they enjoy. Remember, your children are created in the image of God just as you were. They are sinners in need of grace just as you are.

Recommended books: *Helper by* Design by Elyse Fitzpatrick; *The Complete Husband: A Practical Guide to Biblical Husbanding* by Lou Priolo; *What Did You Expect* by Paul David Tripp; *Meaning of Marriage* by Timothy Keller; *Shepherding a Child's Heart* by Tedd Tripp; *Give Them Grace* by Elyse Fitzpatrick and Jessica Thompson.

DAY 30

COLOSSIANS 3:22-4:1

Slaves (bondservants), obey in everything those who are your earthly masters, not by way of eye-service, as people-pleasers, but with sincerity of heart, fearing the Lord. Whatever you do, work heartily, as for the Lord and not for men, knowing that from the Lord you will receive the inheritance as your reward. You are serving the Lord Christ. For the wrongdoer will be paid back for the wrong "he has done, and there is no partiality. Masters, treat your slaves justly and fairly, knowing that you also have a Master in heaven.

As a United States citizen, my understanding of slavery was limited to what I read in history books in school or saw in a movie. When we moved to the Middle East for three years, I experienced more of what slavery looks like. As Westerners, we were treated well as part of the upper class. We had freedom to do most things we would in the States although I will qualify "most things" in the context of our

Christianity. Things that were forbidden weren't things we would be doing anyway.

Where we lived was nine-two percent expats (non-nationals). We experienced a myriad of other cultures many of which did not view all people as equal human beings. I know here in the States this is still an issue too, but I had not personally experienced it to the extent that we did abroad. There were specific cultures and people who treated common workers as sub-human. We witnessed many Westerners who would not behave this way in their own country subscribe to this demeaning, sinful way of regarding others. We had a gardener who told us that at most houses the residents wouldn't even let him fill his water bottle with the sandy water from the hose in the one hundred plus degrees and ninety-five percent humidity. There are other things we thought would be difficult living in the Middle East, but by far this was the most difficult. People gave their pets better drinking water than they would allow the workers to have. This was only one of many degrading manners in which some were regarded.

Paul speaks to slaves and masters, but we can relate the principles to employees and employers. In Paul's day, slaves could include those we would consider professionals. The majority of the population fell into the slave category. It was an accepted practice and a reality in that society. At the writing of Colossians, Onesimus, a runaway slave who came to saving faith, was with Paul (4:9 and the book of Philemon). Paul nor Scripture advocates slavery, but because it was entwined with society, Paul addresses the issue. As Paul's instructions for husbands, wives and parents were counter-cultural, so were his directions to slaves and masters.

"The Bible does not condone slavery any more than it condones polygamy or divorce. Instead, it establishes humane limits for an existing, evil system. ...The law of Moses laid the groundwork for the eventual demise of one of the most demeaning institutions in human society."[53]

Because slavery did exist, Paul instructs how a Christian slave should respond to their human master. They should obey in everything except a command to sin, but Paul elucidates the heart motive behind the obedience. Eye-service describes obedience only when one is being watched. It is strictly external. Obedience is not to please man (fear of man) but is to be out of fear or reverent awe of God. Slaves are pleasing and glorifying God when they obey their earthly masters with a sincere heart.

Verse 23 and 24 elaborate on the motive of working for the Lord and not for men. Colossians 3:18-4:1 deal with horizontal relationships (between us and other people). The godly response to the horizontal relationships stems from our vertical relationship with God. Our identity rests in who we are in Christ and our righteous standing because of His atoning sacrifice. As believers, knowing our grace-position before our true Master, we work all the more heartily. Our approval and reward do not come from man. They come from God (Revelation 20:12-13).

Verse 25 warns that a believer who is not honest, trustworthy, reliable and diligent in his work not only faces consequences from a human master but discipline from God as well. Human masters may show partiality, but God doesn't. On Days 22, 23 and 25 we discussed how the "put ons" are actually living out who we already are. Paul is telling slaves to live in light of who they are in Christ not who they are to the world.

Next Paul turns to masters. He will be sending a now saved Onesimus back to his earthly master Philemon, a believer. In the book of Philemon, Paul will make a plea to Philemon to receive Onesimus with forgiveness and grace as a fellow brother in Christ. There should be a difference in Christian masters. In the body of

Christ, masters and slaves are on equal standing before God. They have the same need before God due to their sin and receive the same grace. They are both made in God's image. Salvation is available to both. Therefore, masters should treat their slaves justly and fairly (Exodus 20:8-10; 21:20, 26-27) knowing that they are real people journeying through life with all that entails, the same as the master.

For Reflection: If you are an employee, are you doing the bare minimum or less at your job? Do you voice disrespect for your boss to others? Do you complain about your situation forgetting that God is sovereign over your work situation? Or are you diligent, trustworthy, reliable and even supportive of your boss as he/she seeks to do their job? Is there a specific action you can take that reflects that your ultimate boss is God?

If you are a boss, do you treat your employees justly and fairly or do you treat them as someone beneath you? Do you acknowledge and give them their due for their good work? Are there ways you can encourage your employees, show them the grace God has given you?

If you are currently unemployed, you can still be diligent, trustworthy and reliable in looking for work, working at things at home or in serving others. For those retired, the same is true for you. Retirement doesn't mean that God is done using you. Even if you are experiencing physical limitations, you can mentor or visit others, send cards, make calls, knit or pray. A friend's sister is mostly confined to bed or her recliner. It can be easy to believe Satan's lies that she is useless, that she can't serve, but she is a mighty prayer warrior. She intercedes before the throne of grace for family and friends throughout each day. This is a precious gift to those she prays for. With God, acts of serving that may seem small or useless to us can be used as big blessings.

DAY 31

COLOSSIANS 4:2-4

*Continue steadfastly in prayer, being watchful in it with thanksgiving.
At the same time, pray also for us, that God may open to us a door
for the word, to declare the mystery of Christ, on account of which I
am in prison—that I may make it clear, which is how I ought to speak.*

Growing up in a Christian home and attending church, I knew I should pray. Knowing and doing or doing successfully (in our minds) are different. I have been too busy to pray. I completely forget about praying. I have been overwhelmed by how much there is to pray for. I feel guilty over sin or that it has been days or months since I took time to pray, so I avoid God. Praying at all times (Ephesians 6:18) or without ceasing (1 Thessalonians 5:17) seems an impossible task. I have felt like I was talking to the air or my teddy bear instead of a real Person. I can't keep my focus for more than thirty seconds. Sometimes I fumble over my words. I'm not eloquent. I wonder if I am following the right formula for prayer. Prayer can seem daunting and even discouraging. It can be one more thing on my daily checklist.

All those thoughts and more have run through my mind regarding prayer over the years. I long for heaven where I will have perfect fellowship with God. No wandering thoughts. No gaps in communicating. No guilt. Just beautiful conversation with my Father.

I had to let go of my expectations of what prayer is supposed to look like. I am reminded of a few lines of a song by Nichole Nordeman called *Holy*. "And all You ever wanted, only me, on my knees, singing holy, holy." God simply wants us to come before the throne of grace, into His presence. He isn't looking for the word perfect, eloquent prayer. He isn't setting His stopwatch to see exactly how much time we spend. He isn't shaking a finger at us because it was a week since we talked to Him last. He is patiently, lovingly waiting for us to come, to bring our burdens, our hurts, our joys, our gratitude, our praise, our requests and our confession.

So, as we delve into today's verses, set aside any apprehension or guilt about prayer. Jesus prayed perfectly in your place. The Spirit intercedes for you when you don't know how to pray (Romans 8:26). You are free to come and talk to your Father.

Paul first instructs the Colossian believers to "continue steadfastly in prayer". Continuing steadfastly is to be devoted or constant to, to courageously persevere. One of my misconceptions about continuous prayer was that I had to actually utter prayers all the time. I think a better way to think of it is as a frame of mind that is always aware of God's presence. As we spend time with Him, dwell on His character and have a greater awareness of His faithful presence, it becomes more and more natural to talk to Him. In that sense, He is familiar and comfortable. As we are going about work or school or parenting, God is present. When trouble comes, we ask God for help. When good things come, we turn to Him in thankfulness. Think of going on a long hike with a friend. You might not have constant dialogue, but they are present, you know it, and they are the first one you turn to and share with because you are very aware that they are there. God is eternally present with us sharing in every moment.

I appreciate the element of perseverance or being devoted to prayer. We don't give up when an immediate answer isn't evident. We don't quit praying because we can't *feel* God's presence. Our persistence isn't to wear God down until He gives in. We persist confident that God is faithful to answer. Richard Trench (1807-1886), archbishop of Dublin put it this way, "Prayer is not overcoming God's reluctance; it is laying hold of His willingness."[54] Isn't that a magnificent picture? God delights in time with us and answering our prayers. He is willing, more than willing to meet with us in prayer. We can meet God with courage not guilt or fear because Jesus made the way for us to boldly, courageously come to God (Hebrews 4:14-16).

Next Paul advises being watchful in prayer. Prayer is the believer's and the Church's great weapon against Satan. In prayer we are trusting our request to the One who alone is able to defeat Satan's schemes, the One who is sovereign over Satan. No wonder Paul uses the word *watchful*. Nehemiah joined prayer and watchfulness as he and the Israelites rebuilt the walls and gates of Jerusalem (Nehemiah 4:9). Jesus told the disciples in the Garden of Gethsemane to "watch and pray" (Mark 14:38). Paul ties prayer and staying alert (Ephesians 6:18). Although being watchful can mean staying awake, the more encompassing meaning is to be alert to specific needs to bring before the Father realizing there is opposition and temptations to distract us.

Third, we come with thanksgiving. If we neglect thanksgiving, we aren't recognizing God as provider and sustainer. Lack of thanksgiving turns our prayers into a selfish wish list. It forgets that we are talking to the Almighty God, not a human Santa Claus. I hope you have been adding to your thankful journal and recognizing how endless the thankful list really is. We will never run out of things to be thankful for if we are willing to look.

In verses 3 and 4, Paul asks the Colossians believers to pray specifically for him and his co-laborers as they share the gospel. I tend to think of Paul as a Super Christian. He was a faithful man of God, but did you catch that he is asking the Colossian believers to pray for him? He isn't so far above them that he doesn't covet their prayers. They aren't second-class prayer warriors, unworthy of praying for him. They are his brothers and sisters in Christ whose prayers are just as sweet to God as Paul's are, just as heard and answered. In fact, God chooses to use the prayers of the saints (that's us!) to empower His Word going forth.

There are several things to glean from Paul's request for prayer. He is not ashamed to ask for prayer and to be specific. His request is for a door (opportunity to share) to be opened for God's Word (1 Corinthians 16:8-9; 2 Corinthians 2:12). Note that he didn't ask for his prison doors to be opened although Paul knew God could do that (Acts 16:26; 12:6-11). Paul did not see his imprisonment as an obstacle to declaring the gospel. It was an opportunity that needed praying for. He had access to the prison guards and beyond (Philippians 1:12-14). Paul's request is for the same gospel that landed him in prison to still be declared. He was single-minded in the ministry God had given him. Finally, Paul did not only ask for an open door to declare the gospel, but that he could declare it in a clear, effective way.

Paul's specific prayer request is a reminder to us as the body of Christ of one way we can pray for pastors and missionaries: that the gospel would be declared clearly even in, or especially in, opposition, trials and persecution.

For Reflection: Have you had similar responses to prayer that I have had? Today is a fresh start to converse with God. Find what works best for you. I have one friend that journals her prayers. I like order, so I created daily cards. Each one has a different attribute of God with songs and a verse that go with it, and then specific groups of people I pray for on that day. For instance, on Mondays, I praise God for His holiness. Then I pray for the church (local and universal), pastors and missionaries. I have specific things to pray for under that as well as the names of the pastors and missionaries we know. I also have cards to pray different aspects of life for my husband each day of the month, and a sheet of Scripture prayers that I pray for a friend each day for a week. This helps me not feel overwhelmed. Over time, I have gotten better at stopping and praying about situations or giving thanks as specific things come up during the day. This helps keep that continuous mindset of prayer (still growing in this).

There are many resources available with Scripture prayers for children, husbands, wives, government leaders, church leaders, etc. Check online or contact me. I'm happy to share.

What works for you may be different and it may vary in different seasons of your life. Moms with newborn or young children are a good example of a different season. They likely do not have the amount of time available that they did before children for prayer and study. Remember, God wants to spend time with you regardless of how that looks.

Take some time today to pray for your pastor and missionaries you know—that they would have opportunities to declare the gospel clearly. There is a great one-month calendar I came across that lists a different aspect to pray for your pastor each day (*Pray For Your Pastor* by Tauna Meyer at ProverbialHomemaker.com for Talking Mom2Mom, Copyright © 2014, All Rights Reserved).

DAY 32

COLOSSIANS 4:5-6

*Conduct yourselves wisely toward outsiders,
making the best use of the time. Let your speech always be
gracious, seasoned with salt, so that you may know how
you ought to answer each person.*

Currently *haters* is a common term often applied to Christians. Even if Christians consistently loved their neighbors and enemies perfectly, there would still be some who would call us haters because we believe and practice what Scripture teaches especially in regard to sin. Sadly, many who bear the name of Christ have not loved their neighbors and enemies. We have often lived hypocritical lives, or we have said and done hateful things. We do not present the Gospel clearly and effectively as Paul desired to do in our verses yesterday.

We often forget that what people need is Jesus, not morality. An unbeliever has no basis or power to obey what Scripture commands apart from Jesus. We put the cart before the horse when we expect unbelievers to live righteously without the transforming power of the Gospel. This is the reason Paul instructs the Colossians to act wisely toward outsiders (unbelievers), make the best use of the time and let their speech be gracious, seasoned with salt. These three points should govern our speech as well.

When Paul beseeches believers to conduct themselves wisely, he is not implying that we must live perfectly. Only Jesus could and did meet that standard. Part of our wise conduct is reflecting Jesus in our actions and words, but the other part is confessing our sin and failure in light of God's grace and forgiveness. We are hypocrites when we have an unrepentant log in our own eye while pointing out the speck in others (Matthew 7:1-5). It's not attractive. In their song "What If I Stumble", DC Talk quoted Brennan Manning, "The greatest single cause of atheism in the world today is Christians: who acknowledge Jesus with their lips, walk out the door, and deny Him by their lifestyle. That is what an unbelieving world simply finds unbelievable."

Wise conduct is discerning how we present the Gospel message. It starts with listening. Hear where the unbeliever is at. Where they hurt. What their objections to God, the Bible and Christianity are. The possibility of them listening to the message of the Gospel increases when we show love and compassion. We can also better know how to bring the Gospel to bear when we know even some of the person's heart.

It is necessary to talk about sin and hell, but wise conduct doesn't do this to the exclusion of grace or vice versa. The unbeliever can't truly fathom the depths of God's grace if they don't know the heinousness of their sin, but at the same time, they need to hear God's grace for the sinner just as we did and continually need to hear. Wise conduct is neither self-righteous (we are more holy than the other) nor silent out of fear of being considered a hater or judgmental. Wise conduct is wise words and actions done in love, humility and truth.

Wise conduct also makes the best use of the time. The Greek *exagorazō* is also translated as *redeem* or to buy up opportunities to witness. Seize them. I am often complacent towards unbelievers. My conduct is unwise, acting as if there is all the time in the world to witness. We don't know how much time each person has. Redeeming the time means we will have an urgency in sharing the Gospel with our words and lives.

In verse 6 Paul elaborates on the speech that characterizes wise conduct. The world's view of Christianity is that it is boring, full of rules, hateful, hypocritical, joyless and/or a crutch. The Gospel is the best news ever. EVER! Our speech should reflect that. It is gracious (*charis* that we have previously studied). According to Strong's Lexicon, it "affords joy, pleasure, delight, sweetness, charm, loveliness." Our speech is seasoned with salt. Just as salt enhances the flavor of food and preserves it from corruption, our speech should bring out the beauty of the Gospel, that it is desirable above all things. Well-seasoned speech blesses those who hear it.

Well-seasoned speech knows how to answer each person. Believers will know how to respond with God's truth. This returns us to Paul's prayer in verses 1:9-10 that believers would be filled with the knowledge of His will in all spiritual wisdom and understanding and increasing in the knowledge of God, and his exhortation in 2:7 of being rooted, built up and established in Christ and what we have been taught.

David Guzik comments on yesterday and today's verses, "This is also an important idea to connect with the earlier passages of Colossians. Paul spent considerable time in this letter explaining the truth and refuting bad doctrine. Yet all the correct knowledge was of little good until it was applied in both the prayer closet and the public street of daily life. We could say that here, Paul genuinely completes his letter."[55]

For Reflection: How would you portray your conduct towards unbelievers? In what ways do you need to reflect God's truth and grace?

Do you have an urgency to share the Gospel with unbelievers or do you forget there may not be a tomorrow? What holds you back from sharing?

How would you depict your speech? Does it display the beauty and gloriousness of the Gospel?

This study is one way you are preparing to answer each person. My prayer is that you continue to grow in your knowledge of God and His will. Be assured that whether your Bible knowledge is great or small, God can use you. It is Him that works through us and in unbelievers to open their eyes and hearts to Him. His work is not dependent on our knowledge. He calls us to be faithful in studying to show ourselves approved (2 Timothy 2:15), redeeming the opportunities and be willing to speak.

DAY 33

COLOSSIANS 4:7-9

Tychicus will tell you all about my activities. He is a beloved brother and faithful minister and fellow servant in the Lord.
I have sent him to you for this very purpose, that you may know how we are and that he may encourage your hearts, and with him Onesimus, our faithful and beloved brother, who is one of you. They will tell you of everything that has taken place here.

If family or a friend is on my mind, I can text, email, Snap Chat, tag in a Facebook or Instagram post or go old school and call or send snail mail. I'm not much of a phone person, but I do enjoy sending snail mail complete with a Suzy's Zoo® sticker on the envelope. No matter which method I choose, I can be in touch with family or friends in seconds or at the most a couple of days. We can take it for granted how easy it is to contact others.

In Paul's time, there weren't smart phones (or any phone). There wasn't even an organized mail carrier system. You couldn't hop a plane, train or automobile and be somewhere in a day or two. Travel was primarily by foot or boat. A letter was hand-delivered via someone you knew traveling in the right direction. Given the sparse communication, it was customary for letters to include personal greetings by many on the sending end not just the writer. Personal instruction to an individual might also be added.

As Paul initiates the close of his letter, we discover the value he placed on the support and encouragement he received from brothers and sisters in Christ. Precious are the faithful friends who stood with Paul through adversity and imprisonment instead of taking the easy way out. Paul was in house arrest in Rome (Acts 28:16). This meant he was dependent on his friends to supply his food and care for his needs. Over the next few days we will meet these friends.

Not much is known about Tychicus. He first comes on the scene in Acts 20:4 as one of Paul's traveling companions through Macedonia. From Acts, we know that he was Asian or possibly from Ephesus (in modern day Turkey). More importantly Paul considered him a beloved brother, faithful minister and fellow servant of the Lord. That is reflected in Paul sending Tychicus to Ephesus (2 Timothy 4:12) and to Titus (Titus 3:12) to labor in his place. Paul not only trusted Tychicus to deliver his letters but to fill in all the details that weren't in his letters to the Colossian and Ephesian churches (Ephesians 6:21). Paul trusted Tychicus to encourage the churches, teach truth and furnish accurate updates from his close relationship with Paul.

Philemon was a believer in Colossae. Onesimus was his runaway slave and an unbeliever when he left Philemon. He encountered Paul in Rome and came to saving faith. By reading Paul's letter to Philemon, we observe Paul's deep love for Onesimus as his son in the faith. Paul's description of Onesimus after a short time of knowing him reveals that Onesimus had already proven himself to Paul. A transformed Onesimus was willing to return to Philemon his master. In his letter to Philemon, Paul entreats Philemon to receive Onesimus as a brother in Christ considering Onesimus' salvation may have been God's purpose when he ran away. Paul is encouraging Philemon to see the bigger, eternal perspective regarding his runaway slave.

For Reflection: With hectic schedules, it can be difficult to sincerely "greet" people, to show concern for someone as individual. Often greeting time at church feels more like a rush to shake hands with as many as possible in the couple minutes allotted. Who can you connect with today? I find that asking how I can pray for someone is one way of showing I indeed care about how they are.

As you think about Tychicus' faithful support to Paul in various ways, identify one or two ways you can encourage and support a church/ministry leader this week.

Further Study: Read Philemon. It's quick and will give you a broader picture of Onesimus.

DAY 34

COLOSSIANS 4:10-11

*Aristarchus my fellow prisoner greets you, and Mark the cousin
of Barnabas (concerning whom you have received instructions—if he
comes to you, welcome him), and Jesus who is called Justus.
These are the only men of the circumcision among my fellow workers
for the kingdom of God, and they have been a comfort to me.*

In today's verses, Paul commends three Jewish co-laborers who were with him. The first is Aristarchus, a native of Thessalonica (Acts 20:4; 27:2). Due to Paul and his companions' teaching regarding the error of human idols, Aristarchus was seized by a rioting mob in Ephesus (Acts 19:29). He traveled with Paul to Jerusalem and Rome (Acts 27:4). In his letter, Paul describes him as a "fellow prisoner." It is likely Aristarchus was not officially a Roman prisoner, but that he chose incarceration to be a benefit and comfort to Paul.

Mark, also known as John Mark, was the author of the Gospel of Mark and the cousin of Barnabas. His mother Mary's home was a gathering place for early Christians (Acts 12:12). We don't know the reason, but Acts 13:13 records that Mark left Paul and company to return to Jerusalem. This later resulted in Paul and Barnabas' disagreement and parting of ways (Acts 15:36-40). That Mark was now back with Paul and Paul was instructing the Colossian believers to welcome him, demonstrates the two were reconciled and co-laborers again.

Warren Wiersbe shares the example found in Mark, "Mark is an encouragement to everyone who has failed in his first attempts to serve God. He did not sit around and sulk. He got back into the ministry and proved himself to the Lord and to the apostle Paul … God used Barnabas to encourage Mark and restore him to service again."[56]

Paul's mention of Justus is the only reference we have to him. He possibly was among the Roman Jewish converts that came to Paul in his imprisonment (Acts 28:23-24). He exemplifies a believer who faithfully serves God without recognition of his deeds.

For Reflection: Aristarchus willingly chose to share Paul's burden of imprisonment. We can share another's burden by sitting with them in the hospital, taking a meal or helping cover chores for someone enduring a trial. Is there someone in your life you could encourage in that way? See Appendix D for additional ideas of ways to help.

Have you been like Mark? Have you given up on a ministry when you should have seen it through or left in a better way? (Note: there are times when God directs us to move on.) Is there someone you need to reconcile with specifically relating to your involvement in a ministry? Be encouraged by Mark's example that God is not done using you.

Is there someone who needs you to be a Barnabas to them, helping restore them to service again?

.

DAY 35

COLOSSIANS 4:12-14

*Epaphras, who is one of you, a servant of Christ Jesus,
greets you, always struggling on your behalf in his prayers,
that you may stand mature and fully assured in all the will of God.
For I bear him witness that he has worked hard for you and
for those in Laodicea and in Hierapolis. Luke the beloved
physician greets you, as does Demas.*

Today we will examine Paul's final three co-laborers who were with him during the writing of Colossian's letter. Paul packs a rich description of Epaphras into a few words. Epaphras is one of the Colossians. It is likely that Epaphras came to saving faith in Ephesus during Paul's three-year ministry there (Acts 19). Epaphras then returned to Colossae to start a church (1:7) as well as evangelize in nearby Laodicea and Hierapolis. It was Epaphras who recognized the false teaching in Colossae and traveled to Rome to obtain Paul's assistance in how to combat it.

Paul calls Epaphras a *servant* or *bondservant* of Christ Jesus. Epaphras and Tychicus are the only other people Paul describes in this way besides Timothy and himself. The Greek *doulos* is used for both an involuntary and voluntary slave. Strong's Lexicon further defines *doulos* metaphorically as "those whose service is used by Christ in extending and advancing His cause among men," and as one who is "devoted to another to the disregard of one's own interests." Epaphras exemplifies this definition by "struggling…in his prayers" for the Colossians (verse 12), working hard for them and coming to Paul for truth against the false teaching.

Paul focuses in on one particular characteristic of Epaphras—his prayer life. Epaphras is the only person that Paul essentially calls a prayer warrior. Prayer was foundational to Epaphras' ministry. There are five keys in how Epaphras prayed demonstrating his deep love for the Colossian believers. First, he prayed always. This manifests Paul's teaching on praying constantly (1:9; 4:2; 1 Thessalonians 5:17). Second, Paul said Epaphras struggled on behalf of the Colossian believers in his prayers. *Agōnizomai* is the same Greek word used to describe Jesus praying in the Garden of Gethsemane. Third, Epaphras was personal in his prayers. Paul said Epaphras prayed "on *your* behalf" (emphasis added).

Fourth, Epaphras prayed specifically—"that you may stand mature and fully assured in all the will of God." This again reflects Paul's prayers and teachings (1:9-10; 1:28; 2:2). Epaphras desired the Colossian believers to grow to completion in Christ (Philippians 1:6) and to know the will of God. Warren Wiersbe responds, "It is not necessary for a believer to drift in life. He can know God's will and enjoy it. As he learns God's will [through Scripture] and lives, he matures in the faith and experiences God's fullness."[57]

Fifth, Epaphras prayed and served sacrificially. Epaphras considered the needs of the church body above his own. Depending on the route, Epaphras' journey from Colossae to Rome to seek Paul's assistance was a minimum of 1332 miles. Today, we would hop a flight and be there in a couple hours, but Epaphras endured a long journey likely by foot and boat. Almost any journey is additional food and travel costs as well as being away from the comfort of home. This is one instance of Epaphras' sacrificial service. From above descriptions, we can conclude he spent much of his time in prayer and serving others not pursuing his own interests.

Luke was a physician. He authored the Gospel of Luke and the book of Acts (together they are approximately one quarter of the New Testament). He was a gentile and probably the only author in the Bible without a Jewish background. Luke traveled with Paul on many of his journeys (identified by his use of "we" in Acts 16:8-17; 20:5-15; 21:1-18; 27:1-28:16) and was with Paul until Paul's death (2 Timothy 4:11). "Luke is a glowing example of the professional man who uses his skills in the service of the Lord and gives himself to go wherever God sends."[58]

Demas does not receive much attention in the Colossians' letter. In Philemon 24, Paul calls him a "fellow worker," so we know he did serve for a time with Paul. However, in 2 Timothy 4:10, we read that Demas deserted Paul because of a love for the present world. That Paul affords only a brief description could be an indication that Demas' divided heart was already evident.

For Reflection: Is there something in Epaphras' prayer life that stands out to you? How can you incorporate it into your prayer life?

God used Luke's style of writing and way of thinking to write two books of the Bible. Although we don't have details, it is probable that Luke used his medical training on the mission field maybe even caring for Paul (Galatians 4:13). How can or are you using the gifts and training God has given you to serve Him?

DAY 36

COLOSSIANS 4:15-18

Give my greetings to the brothers at Laodicea,
and to Nympha and the church in her house. And when this letter
has been read among you, have it also read in the church
of the Laodiceans; and see that you also read the letter
from Laodicea. And say to Archippus, "See that you fulfill the ministry
that you have received in the Lord." I, Paul, write this greeting
with my own hand. Remember my chains. Grace be with you.

You've made it to the final day of our journey together through Colossians. Paul pens a few parting greetings and personal instructions to finish his letter.

Paul greets the brothers at Laodicea and asks that the Colossian and Laodicean believers exchange the letters Paul sent to each of them. Theologians have speculated about the letter to the Laodiceans, but nothing is known for sure. We know only that the letters to the Colossians and Laodiceans consisted of relevant information for both churches and that Paul desired them to be shared. It was a means for Paul in his absence to teach multiple churches.

Nympha is another unknown. Some manuscripts have the masculine form of the name. This is not a point for division. Rather, focus on the church in an individual's home. The early church did not have their own, special buildings. Believers met in someone's home. Small. Intimate. Everyone knew everybody else. It was not until the third century that churches began to meet in their own buildings.

Archippus is thought to be Philemon's son and a pastor possibly of the Laodicean church (Philemon 2) although we don't know for certain where his ministry was. Paul doesn't charge Archippus directly. He is calling on the Colossian and Laodicean believers to repeat his words to Archippus. We can only speculate why Paul did this. Archippus may have needed to hear it from the church body so he would know they wanted his ministry to them or to remind him of the seriousness of his calling.

Paul's charge to Archippus is akin to his exhortation to Timothy (2 Timothy 4:5). Archippus is to *fulfill* his ministry. The Greek conveys the concept of God's distinct purposes for believers to carry out (Ephesians 2:10). Archippus, as a pastor, was called to teach God's word. That is what he was to faithfully fulfill.

Over the years, some people have thought Paul's words were a rebuke to Archippus. Adam Clarke responds, "It is more likely, therefore, that the words of the apostle convey no censure, but are rather intended to stir him up to further diligence, and to encourage him in the work, seeing he had so much false doctrine and so many false teachers to contend with."[59]

In light of Paul's closing words in Colossians as well as in some of his other letters, we conclude that Paul dictated to a scribe and signed it himself for authentication (1 Corinthians 16:21; Galatians 6:11; 2 Thessalonians 3:17).

His final instruction is for the Colossian believers to remember his chains. In Ephesians 1:16, Paul ties remembering to prayer. So, his reminder here in verse 18 is a likely an appeal for the Colossian believers to pray for him in his imprisonment whether for his release or his opportunities to share the gospel while in chains (4:3).

As Paul often began and ended his letters, he prayed for grace to be with the Colossian believers. Believers need God's grace every day in our sanctification, but this was a special encouragement to the church at Colossae as they fought against the false teaching of works-righteousness. Grace alone through faith alone in Christ alone.

For Reflection: Take time today to pray for those in the persecuted church. The Voice of the Martyrs ministry is a good resource for how to pray, current persecution in the world and ways to aid those affected by persecution.

Flip back through our journey in Philippians. What were some of the highlights for you personally?

APPENDIX A

QUESTIONS FOR SMALL GROUPS

If you would like to use this devotional for your Small Group, I suggest each person do the daily devotions for the week on their own. You can use the below questions for your weekly time together. Select questions are pulled from the daily Reflections, but feel free to use any of the daily Reflection questions.

Week 1 (Days 1-7)

1. What was your main take away from the past week?

2. How would you describe your current spiritual growth? (Day 3)

3. Who has been a faithful Epaphras in your life? Why? (Day 3)

4. What is hindering fruit in your life (Hebrews 12:1)? Is there a specific fruit of the Spirit that might need intentional cultivating? (Day 5)

5. What are things are thankful for? (Day 6)

6. How does Jesus' preeminence impact your perspective on a current circumstance?

Group Praise: Use answers from Questions 3 and 5 to praise and thank God in your group prayer time.

Group Prayer: Use answers from Questions 2 and 4 to pray for each other.

Week 2 (Days 8-14)

1. What was your main take away from the past week?

2. How does Jesus holding all the details of your life together (or every created thing) encourage you specifically? (Day 8)

3. What in Jesus do you adore or leaves you in awe? (Day 9)

4. Would you describe your faith as stable, steadfast and not shifting from the hope you have in the gospel? Or is this a period of struggle? Why is it stable or a struggle? (Day 11)

5. Who is a person (don't have to share the name) that you regularly have an opportunity to offer Biblical counsel to? Share what ways you came up with to be intentional with this person or have the group help you with ideas. (Day 13)

6. Do you see Jesus and the wisdom and knowledge hidden in Him as a treasure? What hinders you acting on this truth or delighting in time in God's Word? (Day 14)

Group Praise: Use answers from Questions 3 and 4 to praise and thank God in your group prayer time.

Group Prayer: Use answers from 4, 5 and 6 to pray for each other.

Week 3 (Days 15-21)

1. What was your main take away from the past week?

2. Share what has worked for you in your quiet time? What do you enjoy? (Day 15)

3. Share something you have been learning in your quiet time? (Day 15)

4. What in your life have you made into Jesus plus _____? What trust transfer needs to happen? (Day 16 and 19)

5. Are there specific areas you are succumbing to Satan's condemnation? (Day 18)

6. What earthly things do you tend to set your mind on? Are you fearing man or circumstances rather than God? What results of this do you observe in your life?

7. What truths do you need to set your mind on? What attributes of God would be encouraging to remember? What certainties of your position in Christ alter your perspective?

Group Praise: Use answers from Questions 3 to praise and thank God in your group prayer time.

Group Prayer: Use answers from 4, 5 and 6 to pray for each other.

Week 4 (Days 22-28)

1. What was your main take away from the past week?

2. What aspect of your identity in Christ are you most thankful for? (Day 23)

3. What things consume you? (Day 23)

4. How have you been tempted to discriminate? (Day 25)

5. Did any of the graces to put on in Colossians 3:12-13 stand out to you? Why? Which ones do you struggle with the most? Why? (Day 26)

Group Praise: Use answers from Questions 2 to praise and thank God in your group prayer time.

Group Prayer: Use answers from 3, 4 and 5 to pray for each other.

Week 5 (Days 29-35)

1. What was your main take away from the past week?

2. Use the questions from Day 29 that are appropriate for your small group (i.e. wives/women, husbands/men, children or parents.

3. Share prayer practices that have been good for you.

4. Do you have an urgency to share the gospel or to pray for unbelievers? What holds you back? (Day 32)

5. Is there something in Epaphras' prayer life that stands out to you? How can you incorporate it into your prayer life?

Group Praise: This week we considered people Paul was thankful for in his life and ministry. Thank God for co-laborers in ministry that you are thankful for.

Group Prayer: Use answers from 2 and 4 to pray for each other.

Week 6 (Day 36 and summary) or you can incorporate this into your Week 5.

1. What impacted you the most in this Journey Through Colossians?

2. What changes in your life are you already seeing as you have applied principles you have learned?

Group Praise: Use answers from Questions 1 and 2 to praise and thank God in your group prayer time.

Group Prayer: Take time to pray together for those in the persecuted church. (Day 36)

APPENDIX B

"IN HIM TRUTHS"

Read through the book of Colossians looking for any phrases of "in Him/Christ", "with Him/Christ," "through Him/Christ," or similar phrases depending on your translation. You might want to circle or underline them. In the chart below, list the phrase and then what the blessings are that we have in Christ. This a great reminder of just a few blessings we have to be thankful and encouraged by.

Verse	In Him, With Him, Through Him	Blessing that comes through who we are in Him.
1:4	Your faith in Christ Jesus	Christ is sufficient. Faith in Christ's work is enough. We don't need anything added.

APPENDIX C

PRAYERS FROM COLOSSIANS

I thank God, the Father of our Lord Jesus Christ, when I pray for _____, since I heard of their faith in Christ Jesus and of the love that they have for all the saints, because of the hope laid up for them in heaven. (1:3-5a)

I ask that _____ may be filled with the knowledge of His will in all spiritual wisdom and understanding, so as to walk in a manner worthy of the Lord, fully pleasing to Him, bearing fruit in every good work and increasing in the knowledge of God. May _____ be strengthened with all power, according to His glorious might, for all endurance and patience with joy, giving thanks to the Father, who has qualified him/her to share in the inheritance of the saints in light. (1:9-12)

Father, help _____ to continue in the faith, stable and steadfast, not shifting from the hope of the gospel that he/she has heard. (1:23)

Let _____'s heart be encouraged, being knit together in love, to reach all the riches of full assurance of understanding and the knowledge of God's mystery, which is Christ in whom are hidden all the treasures of wisdom and knowledge. Let him/her not be deluded with plausible arguments. (2:2-4)

As _____ has received Christ Jesus the Lord, let him/her walk in Him, rooted and built up in Him and established in the faith, just as he/she was taught, abounding in thanksgiving. Help him/her not be taken captive by philosophy and empty deceit, according to human tradition, according to the elemental spirits of the world, and not according to Christ. (2:6-8)

May _____ seek the things that are above, where Christ is, seated at the right hand of God. Let him/her set his/her mind on things that are above, not on things that are on earth. (3:1-2)

Father, let _____ put to death what is earthly in himself/herself and put on his/her new self, which is being renewed in knowledge after the image of its creator. Let _____ put on, as God's chosen ones, holy and beloved, compassion, kindness, humility, meekness, and patience, bearing with one another, and forgiving each other as the Lord has forgiven him/her (3:5-13)

Let _____ put on love, which binds everything together in perfect harmony. And let the peace of Christ rule in his/her heart, to which indeed he/she was called to one body. And be thankful. (3:14-15)

Lord, let the word of Christ dwell in _____ richly, teaching and admonishing one another in all wisdom, singing psalms and hymns and spiritual songs, with thankfulness in their heart to You. (3:16)

Father, whatever _____ does, in word or deed, let everything be done in the name of the Lord Jesus, giving thanks to God the Father through Him. (3:17)

Let _____ submit to her husband, as is fitting the Lord (or let _____ love his wife and not be harsh with her). (3:18 or 19)

Let _____ work heartily in whatever he/she does, as for the Lord and not for men, knowing that from the Lord he/she will receive the inheritance as his/her reward. (3:23-24)

Father, let _____ continue steadfastly in prayer, being watchful in it with thanksgiving. (4:2)

Let _____ conduct himself/herself wisely toward outsiders, making the best use of the time. Let his/her speech always be gracious, seasoned with salt, so that he/she may know how he/she ought to answer each person. (4:5-6)

Father, may _____ stand mature and fully assured in all the will of God. (4:12)

APPENDIX D

SONGS FOR COLOSSIANS

I have tried to put the original information for each song. You may have a particular artist and version that you like best. I do!

Baloche, Paul. "All Hail the Power of Jesus' Name." Light the Nation With Prayer. 1999.

Big Daddy Weave. "Alive." When the Light Comes. 2019.

Chapman, Steven Curtis. "We Believe." Worship and Believe. 2016.

Chapman, Steven Curtis. "One True God." Worship and Believe. 2016.

Chapman, Steven Curtis. "What Kind of Joy." For the Sake of the Call. 1990.

Crosby, Fanny. "Redeemed, How I Love to Proclaim It." Public Domain.

Daigle, Lauren. "How Can It Be." How Can It Be. 2015.

Getty, Keith & Kristyn. "The Perfect Wisdom of Our God." Hymns for the Christian Life. 2012.

Grant, Amy. "This Is My Father's World." Legacy...Hymns and Faith. 2002.

Grant, Amy. "Thy Word." Straight Ahead. 1984.

Klinkenberg, David. "Immortal, Invisible." Legacy Hymns of Our Heritage. 2007.

MercyMe. "Best News Ever." Lifer. 2017.

MercyMe. "Word of God Speak." Spoken For. 2002.

Newsboys. "We Believe." Restart. 2013.

Newsboys. "You Hold It All (Every Mountain)." Love Riot. 2016.

Petra. "Show Your Power." Petra Praise 2: We Need Jesus. 1997.

Powell, Mac. "And Can It Be." Love Divine: The Songs of Charles Wesley. 2010.

Praise Band. "He Is Able." WOW Worship Orange. 1999.

Rice, Chris. "A Mighty Fortress Is Our God." Peace Like a River: The Hymns Project. 2007.

Rodriguez, Chris. "Mighty Is Our God." WOW Worship Blue. 1989

Smith, Michael W. "Above All." Worship. 2001.

Smith, Michael W. "Breathe." Worship. 2002.

Sovereign Grace Churches. "Totally God, Totally Man." The Ology: Ancient Truths Ever New. 2015.

Sovereign Grace Churches. "Our Song From Age to Age." From Age To Age. 2012.

Sovereign Grace Churches. "You Stand Alone." Sooner Count the Stars: Worshiping the Triune God. 2015.

Third Day. "Show Me Your Glory." Offerings II: All I Have To Give. 2003.

Tomlin, Chris. "Indescribable." Arriving. 2004.

Townsend, Stuart. "Speak O Lord." Creation Sings. 2009.

LeBlanc, Charlie and Hosanna Music. "Christ in You." To Him Who Sits on the Throne. 1986.

Watermark. "More Than You'll Ever Know." All Things New. 2000.

APPENDIX E

BEARING ONE ANOTHER'S BURDENS

The following is part of the Love in Action ministry
at my church, Lolo Community Church, designed to encourage the
church body in ways we can bear one another's burdens.

Romans 12:10,13 *"Love one another with brotherly affection. Outdo one another in showing honor…Contribute to the needs of the saints and seek to show hospitality."*

As a church family, we are to help carry each other's burdens, but sometimes we don't know how to be helpful. Many of those in a struggle will not want to ask for help. Below we have some ideas of things you could ask them specifically if they would be a help or things you can just do. Just because the person may have family members nearby does not mean that they don't need additional help. Caring for a loved one can be overwhelming at times.

We also want to remember those with long-term illnesses. We can still be a blessing to them even if it is not a crisis time.

Finally, part of bearing each other's burdens is also being willing to share when we need help. This isn't always easy, but we don't want to hinder others using their gifts to be a blessing.

A good rule to think of when trying to care for others is to consider what has been a blessing to you during a time of need.

WAYS TO BE A BLESSING…

All Situations

- Pray with the person
- Meals
- Getting groceries or running errands
- Laundry
- Cleaning
- Rides particularly for doctor visits
- Restaurant gift cards to places with delivery or take-out.
- Visiting at the hospital or at home (many get lonely)
- Paper goods (to eliminate dish washing)
- Cards
- Lawn mowing or snow removal (co-ordinate with deacons who try to cover this)

Surgery, Chemo or Extended Hospital Stay

- Coupons/gift card for hospital cafeteria for the family of the one in the hospital
- Lap shawls
- Death In the Family

- Cleaning clothes for the service or home before guests.
- Set-up or clean-up for service
- Food for service

Families With Kids

- Babysit
- Drive kids to school or activities

DID YOU LIKE THIS BOOK?

Consider writing a review on Amazon or Goodreads.

Also available on Amazon.com or BookBaby.com

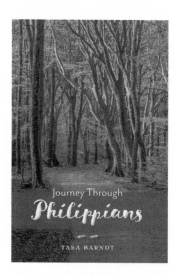

tarabarndt.wixsite.com/journeythrough

 /Tara Barndt

 @tarabarndt

END NOTES

1 Bridges, Jerry, *Transforming Grace: Living Confidently in God's Unfailing Love* (Colorado Springs, CO: NavPress).

2 Orr, Katie, *Everyday Love: Bearing Witness to His Purpose* (Birmingham, AL: New Hope Publishers).

3 Moo, Douglas J, *The Letters to the Colossians and to Philemon* (Grand Rapids, MI: Wm. B. Eerdmans Publishing Co. 2008).

4 Tripp, Paul David, *Awe: Why It Matters For Everything We Think, Say, & Do* (Wheaton, IL: Crossway) pg. 47

5 Tripp, Paul David, *Awe: Why It Matters For Everything We Think, Say, & Do* (Wheaton, IL: Crossway) pg. 49

6 Wiersbe, Warren, Colossians: *Be Complete, Become the Whole Person God Intended You to Be* (Colorado Springs, CO: David C Cook).

7 O'Brien, Peter T., *Word Biblical Commentary, Volume 44, Colossians, Philemon* (Nashville, TN: Thomas Nelson Publishers), pg. 22

8 Spurgeon, Charles. *Spurgeon's Sermons Volume 29* (London, UK: Passmore & Alabaster).

9 Bruce, F.F., *The Epistles to the Colossians, to Philemon, and to the Ephesians (The New International Commentary on the New Testament* (Grand Rapids, MI: B. Eerdmans Publishing Co.).

10 Spurgeon, Charles, *Morning and Evening: The Classical Daily Devotional* (Uhrichsville, OH: Barbour Books).

11 Tripp, Paul David, *Awe: Why It Matters For Everything We Think, Say, & Do* (Wheaton, IL: Crossway)

12 Voskamp, Ann, *One Thousand Gifts Devotional* (Grand Rapids, MI: Zondervan).

13 Sproul. R.C., (19 July 2019) Radio Interview: *Ask R.C. Live event with R.C. Sproul*, https://www.ligonier.org/learn/qas/how-important-are-creeds-and-confessions/

14 Sproul, R.C. Jr., "What is the Function of Creeds." RCSproulJr.com, 28 March 2015, https://www.ligonier.org/blog/what-function-creeds/

15 Robertson, A.T. (Greek scholar), Quoted in *Study Guide for Colossians 1* by David Guzik, studylight.org

16 Wiersbe, Warren, *Colossians: Be Complete, Become the Whole Person God Intended You to Be* (Colorado Springs, CO: David C Cook).

17 Clarke, Adam, *Christian Theology: Selected From His Published and Unpublished Writings* (Lane & Scott, 1851).

18 Ligonier Ministries, "The True Firstborn of Israel." *Tabletalk Magazine.* January 2011. https://tabletalkmagazine.com/daily-study/2011/01/true-firstborn-israel/

19 Daigle, Lauren. "How Can It Be." How Can It Be. 2015.

20 Spurgeon, Charles. *Metropolitan Tabernacle Pulpit Volume 17.* (London, England: Forgotten Books).

21 Jones, Mark. *God Is: A Devotional Guide to the Attributes of God.* (Wheaton, IL: Crossway).

22 Strong, James. Strong's Exhaustive Concordance of the Bible. Abingdon Press, 1890. Print.

23 Ligonier Ministries, "Proclaiming Christ." *Tabletalk Magazine*. January 2011. https://tabletalkmagazine.com/daily-study/2011/01/proclaiming-christ/

24 Ligonier Ministries, "All The Treasures of God's Wisdom." *Tabletalk Magazine*. December 2015. https://tabletalkmagazine.com/daily-study/2015/12/all-treasures-gods-wisdom/

25 Ligonier Ministries, "Walking In Christ Jesus." *Tabletalk Magazine*. February 2011. https://tabletalkmagazine.com/daily-study/2011/02/walking-christ-jesus/

26 Beermer, Britt and Ham, Ken, "Already Gone Part 1: An Epidemic on Our Hands." Answers in Genesis. October 2000 and May 2017. https://answersingenesis.org/christianity/church/already-gone/

27 The Banner of Truth Trust (2018). *The Heidelberg Catechism*. New York: Charles Scribner.

28 Zondervan (2014). *The Creeds: Reflections and Scripture on the Apostles' and Nicene Creeds*. Grand Rapids, MI: Zondervan.

29 MacArthur, John, *Colossians and Philemon: Completion and Reconciliation in Christ*. (Nashville, TN: Nelson Books).

30 Jones, Mark, *A Devotional Guide to the Attributes of God*. (Wheaton, IL: Crossway).

31 The Banner of Truth Trust (2018). *The Heidelberg Catechism*. New York: Charles Scribner.

32 Spurgeon, Charles, *Morning and Evening, The Classic Daily Devotional*. (Uhrichsville, OH: Barbour Publishing, Inc.). November 8, morning.

33 Wiersbe, Warren, *Colossians: Be Complete, Become the Whole Person God Intended You to Be* (Colorado Springs, CO: David C Cook).

34 Guzik, David, *Philippians & Colossians Verse By Verse Commentary* (EnduringWord.com).

35 Sproul, R.C., *St. Andrew's Expositional Commentary on Romans*. (Wheaton, IL: Crossway).

36 Wiersbe, Warren, *Colossians: Be Complete, Become the Whole Person God Intended You to Be* (Colorado Springs, CO: David C Cook).

37 Wright, N. T., *Colossians and Philemon.* (Downers Grove, IL: InterVarsity Press, USA).

38 Orr, Katie, *Everyday Obedience: Walking Purposefully in His Grace.* (Birmingham, AL: New Hope Publishers).

39 Wiersbe, Warren, *Colossians: Be Complete, Become the Whole Person God Intended You to Be* (Colorado Springs, CO: David C Cook).

40 MacArthur, John, *Colossians and Philemon: Completion and Reconciliation in Christ.* (Nashville, TN: Nelson Books).

41 Orr, Katie, *Everyday Obedience: Walking Purposefully in His Grace.* (Birmingham, AL: New Hope Publishers).

42 Jones, Robert D., *Anger: Calming Your Heart* (Philiipsburg, NJ: P&R Publishing).

43 Orr, Katie, *Everyday Obedience: Walking Purposefully in His Grace.* (Birmingham, AL: New Hope Publishers).

44 Sproul, R. C. (Ed.), (2005). In *The Reformation Study Bible* (p. 1733). Orlando, FL: Ligonier Ministries.

45 O, Brien, Peter T., *Word Biblical Commentary, Volume 44, Colossians, Philemon* (Nashville, TN: Thomas Nelson Publishers), pg. 199.

46 Tripp, Paul David, *Awe: Why It Matters For Everything We Think, Say, & Do* (Wheaton, IL: Crossway).

47 Tripp, Paul David, *Whiter Than Snow: Meditations on Sin and Mercy.* (Wheaton, IL: Crossway).

48 Tripp, Paul David & Lane, Timothy S., *Instruments in the Redeemer's Hands: How to Help Others Change.* (Greensboro, NC: New Growth Press).

49 Wiersbe, Warren, *Colossians: Be Complete, Become the Whole Person God Intended You to Be* (Colorado Springs, CO: David C Cook).

50 Guzik, David. "Colossians," David Guzik: Study Guide for Colossians 3. https://www.blueletterbible.org/Comm/guzik_david/StudyGuide2017-Col/Col-3.cfm (accessed November 4, 2019).

51 Guzik, David. "Colossians," David Guzik: Study Guide for Colossians 3. https:// www.blueletterbible.org/Comm/guzik_david/StudyGuide2017-Col/Col-3.cfm (accessed November 5, 2019).

52 Wiersbe, Warren, *Colossians: Be Complete, Become the Whole Person God Intended You to Be* (Colorado Springs, CO: David C Cook).

53 *The Apologetics Study Bible* (Nashville, TN: Holman Bible Publishers).

54 Wiersbe, Warren, *Colossians: Be Complete, Become the Whole Person God Intended You to Be* (Colorado Springs, CO: David C Cook).

55 Guzik, David. "Colossians," David Guzik: Study Guide for Colossians 3. https://www.blueletterbible.org/Comm/guzik_david/StudyGuide2017-Col/Col-4. cfm?a=1111006 (accessed November, 19, 2019).

56 Wiersbe, Warren, *Colossians: Be Complete, Become the Whole Person God Intended You to Be* (Colorado Springs, CO: David C Cook).

57 Wiersbe, Warren, *Colossians: Be Complete, Become the Whole Person God Intended You to Be* (Colorado Springs, CO: David C Cook).

58 Wiersbe, Warren, *Colossians: Be Complete, Become the Whole Person God Intended You to Be* (Colorado Springs, CO: David C Cook).

59 Clarke, Adam. "Colossians," David Guzik: Study Guide for Colossians 4. https://www.blueletterbible.org/Comm/guzik_david/StudyGuide2017-Col/Col-4. cfm?a=1111001